HOW FIGURE SKATING WORKS

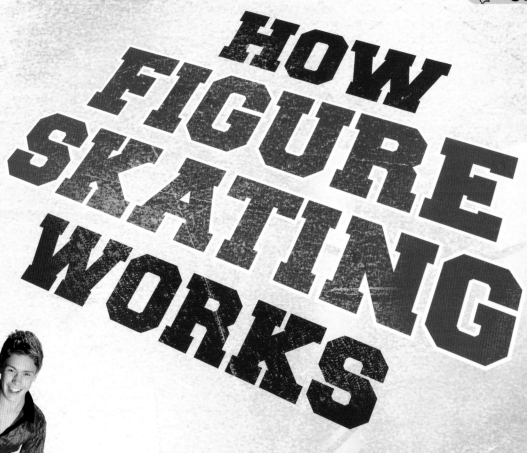

Keltie Thomas

Illustrations by Stephen MacEachern

MAPLE TREE PRESS

Maple Tree Press books are published by Owlkids Books Inc.
10 Lower Spadina Avenue, Suite 400, Toronto, Ontario M5V 2Z2
www.owlkids.com

Text © 2009 Keltie Thomas
Illustrations © 2009 Stephen MacEachern

Distributed in Canada by Raincoast Books
9050 Shaughnessy Street, Vancouver, British Columbia V6P 6E5

Distributed in the United States by Publishers Group West
1700 Fourth Street, Berkeley, California 94710

Dedication
For figure skating fans everywhere

Acknowledgments
Many thanks to all the wonderful people at Maple Tree Press and Owlkids,
Roger Yip, James Hackland, Trennt Michaud, Chelsea Saunders, Lisa Fralick,
Michelle Fralick, Benzie Sangma, Ice Galaxy, Karen Cover, World Skating Museum,
Jimmie Santee, Professional Skaters Association, John Crossingham, Deb Yea.

Cataloguing in Publication Data

Thomas, Keltie
How figure skating works / Keltie Thomas ;
illustrated by Stephen MacEachern.

ISBN 978-1-897349-58-8 (bound).--ISBN 978-1-897349-59-5 (pbk.)
1. Figure skating--Juvenile literature. I. MacEachern, Stephen II. Title.
GV850.4.T46 2009   j796.91'2   C2009-901000-3

Library of Congress Control Number: 2009923344

Design and illustration: Stephen MacEachern
Photo Credits: see page 64

Canada Council   Conseil des Arts   ONTARIO ARTS COUNCIL
for the Arts   du Canada   CONSEIL DES ARTS DE L'ONTARIO

We acknowledge the financial support of the Canada Council for the Arts, the Ontario
Arts Council, the Government of Canada through the Book Publishing Industry
Development Program (BPIDP), and the Government of Ontario through the Ontario
Media Development Corporation's Book Initiative for our publishing activities.

Printed in China

A   B   C   D   E   F

CONTENTS

Chapter 1

Chapter 2

Chapter 3

HOW DOES FIGURE SKATING WORK?

Fans, skaters, and inquiring minds everywhere want to know!

What makes figure skating one of the most exciting and skilled sports on Earth? Why do some figure skaters soar in competition and others fall apart all over the ice? What makes the ice so slippery? How do skaters jump up, turn around four times in the air, then land on one foot while skating backward? And which jump is which? Do skaters get dizzy when they spin? What do the judges look for as they mark skaters? And just who are the judges anyway?

Well, just like everything else on Earth, the answers all come down to science—plus a few things science hasn't managed to explain yet! And if you think that makes figure skating sound boring, you'd better check what planet you're on. But, hey, why don't you check out the world of figure skating in action for yourself? Whether you want answers to those burning questions, tips on becoming a better skater, the scoop on inside information, or just to have a blast with your skates, this book's for you.

Patrick Chan

HEY! YOU DON'T HAVE TO BE A FIGURE SKATING MANIAC TO READ THIS BOOK. THE RULES, REGS, AND LINGO OF SKATING ARE DECODED ON PAGE 61.

Michelle Kwan

Nancy Kerrigan and Tonya Harding

Why Is Figure Skating So Fascinating?

More people watched the 1994 Olympic figure skating competition than any event in Olympic history. Maybe that's because the skate-off between Nancy Kerrigan and Tonya Harding bubbled over with more bizarre plot twists than a soap opera. It all began off the ice at the U.S. championships, when an attacker struck Nancy hard on the knee with a metal baton. In her absence, Tonya won the U.S. title.

Then police arrested none other than Tonya's bodyguard. He said that Tonya's ex-husband had planned the attack! Eventually, she would admit she knew of the plan all along. Tonya was banned from skating for life, but not before she and Nancy competed at the Olympics—where they had to share practice ice! Tonya fell apart in the short program, missing the landings on her jumps, and lost any hope of a medal.

Meanwhile, Nancy nailed all her jumps, turning in a near-perfect performance. But during the long program, Oksana Baiul burst Nancy's bubble. The Ukrainian skated off with a highly controversial gold-medal win. The nine judges were split—five felt Oksana won, while four thought Nancy was the best. Some still say that Nancy was robbed. In figure skating, what happens off the ice can be just as fascinating as the on-ice action!

Chapter 1

SKATING ON THIN ICE

Swish! Swish! Figure skaters push with one foot then the other, zipping down the ice at top speed. They jab a toe pick in the ice and jump up, up, and away, twirling around three times in midair. Then they come back down, landing on the ice with one foot.

Swick! They spiral, extending one leg straight out behind them in a long glide across the ice. They fly into spins, turning round and round on the spot. And sometimes, they slip—oops!—and fall. Wham! So what makes figure skating such a fluid, exciting, and risky sport? The ice, of course!

The ice may be slippery, but it also helps skaters glide and spin on the spot. When any two objects rub against each other, they create friction, a force that slows them down. But when a skate blade rubs against ice, this smooth surface cuts down the friction. Ice gives figure skaters more speed and fluid movement than anything else on Earth. Check out the slippery science of ice.

Chill out!

Hey Ice, It's Been a Slice!

 hat makes ice such a smooth character to skate on?

It's way cool

You need a big chill to freeze water into ice. The world's first skating rinks formed naturally on ponds and lakes in the winter when the temperature dipped to 0°C (32°F) or below. And once the temperature rose, the ice melted and disappeared. Skaters were at the mercy of winter's unpredictable freezes and thaws. What's more, snowdrifts piled up on natural ice rinks and strong winds often blew skaters about. Skating depended entirely on the elements until refrigeration was invented in 1859 and ice could be kept indoors. The world's first indoor rinks soon followed and skating became cool in more ways than one.

It's slippery

Just what makes ice so slippery has puzzled experts for more than 150 years. Some scientists thought that skates slip on ice because pressure from the blades melts a thin layer on the surface into water. The blades then glide across the water, which then refreezes almost instantly. Others said friction created between the blades and the ice as they rub against each other gives off heat that melts into a thin layer of water. But they were both wrong! With more research, they discovered that the pressure from skate blades isn't enough to melt ice in extremely cold temperatures, while melting from friction doesn't explain why you can slip when standing still!

It wears a slick jacket

In the 1990s, scientists finally cracked the slippery case of why objects slide and glide on ice. They found evidence that a thin waterlike jacket covers the entire surface of ice. What's more, even though water freezes into ice at 0°C (32°F), they discovered that ice still wears this water coating at temperatures as low as -129°C (-200°F)! Scientists think this slick coating forms on ice because oxygen atoms in ice vibrate—or shake around—more at the surface than inside. But not all scientists agree, so the slippery case of ice is anything but closed.

IT'S ABNORMAL

Ever noticed how ice floats in water? That's not normal behavior—in fact, most solids sink in liquids of the same substance. That's because most substances are denser as a solid than as a liquid. But ice—which is frozen, or solid, water—is actually less dense than water, so it floats! If ice behaved like a normal solid, skating might never have happened on Earth. The world's first skating rinks would have sunk straight to the bottom of the lake! So people might never have invented skates. Who knew the origins of skating were a little bit dense?

IT'S BLUE

The ice for figure skating competitions isn't clear or even white. According to the U.S. Figure Skating Association, it has to be "TV blue," which looks better on TV than the natural color of ice. So when competition ice is made, icemakers mix a liquid blue paint with water and spray it on the ice. The ice is blue? Who knew!?

IT'S PURE

Figure skating ice isn't made with any old tap water. It's pure water. Expert icemakers use water that's free of impurities and minerals. Why? That way the ice is clear rather than cloudy, less dirt builds up, and there's less friction between the skate blades and the surface. Believe it or not, experts can tell if ice has been made with pure water just by looking at it.

TRY THIS!

Want to see the slippery character of ice in action?

Try this experiment and see what happens when two pieces of ice come into contact for a while.

YOU WILL NEED

- two ice cubes
- a small jar or eggcup
- rocks

1 Place the ice cubes in the jar so the cubes touch and remain in contact.

2 If necessary, place rocks around the ice cubes to help keep the cubes touching.

3 Place the jar in the freezer overnight.

4 Take the jar and cubes out of freezer. What do you notice about the cubes?

What does this reveal about the nature of ice?

Answer on page 64.

Skate Bite

The ice you skate on is only one kind of ice. Scientists think there are about a dozen other kinds of ice. Some kinds may even keep their cool in the hot interior of the Earth.

THE RINK

Skaters arrive at the rink about a week before a big competition to get a feel for the ice. Making ice as smooth as glass for figure skating is no easy job. Poor ice conditions—slushy, choppy, or hard ice—can be the talk of the competition for all the wrong reasons! Depending on the rink, making ice from scratch can take anywhere from 24 hours to a couple of days. Here's how it's done.

Skate Bite

It takes about 90,910 L (24,015 gal.) of water to make 5 cm (2 in.) of ice for a figure skating competition. That would fill 910 bathtubs!

1 The ice-making crew cools the rink to about 16°C (61°F).

4 A paint truck sprays pure water onto the slab to make a layer of ice that will stick to the slab. When this freezes, more water is sprayed on to make a second layer of ice.

5 The crew drives the paint truck over the ice. It sprays the ice evenly with "TV blue" paint.

2 The crew builds ice on a concrete floor called the ice slab. Freezing saltwater flows through pipes in the slab to cool it to 0°C (32°F). Insulation under the slab stops the ground temperature from affecting the ice.

3 A layer of heated concrete stops the ice from freezing the ground below, which could damage the rink building. The rink sits on a layer of sand and gravel that has a groundwater drain.

6 The crew seals the paint with a layer of ice 1/16th of an inch thick. After this layer freezes, they use hoses to add 16 to 20 more layers, one at a time. This process makes better ice.

Ice Slab

Insulation

Heated Concrete

Refrigeration System

Sand and Gravel Base

Ground Water Drain

7 The ice is ready for skaters when it's 5 cm (2 in.) thick.

THICK AND THIN

Ask an elite figure skater and a pro hockey player what makes "good ice" and you'll get two very different answers. Hockey players like "fast ice," which is hard, so they can skate and pass the puck swiftly. Fast ice is about -8°C (18°F), but figure skaters prefer warmer "slow ice"—it's -4.5°C (24°F). This ice is softer so their blades can grip it more easily and it has more "give." Figure skaters say that slow ice cushions their landings. Figure skaters also use ice that is a whole 2 cm (1 in.) thicker than hockey ice. This extra thickness adds more than just cushioning—it also ensures that skaters don't hit their toe picks on the concrete under the ice as they take off for jumps.

KEEPING ITS COOL

Once it's made, keeping the ice cool is like trying to store a giant ice cube in a freezer that's full of holes and hot air. The rink doors are constantly opening and closing. During skating performances and competitions, hot TV lights beam down on the ice, and the body heat of thousands of fans surrounds it. A crew of engineers works with some high-tech tools to do the job. Sensors in the ice slab measure the temperature at the bottom of the ice, while an infrared camera 40 m (132 ft.) above the ice records its surface temperature. The engineers check these readings on a computer, and tell the refrigeration system to chill out or warm up the ice as needed.

Skate Bite

One day, figure skaters may skate on fake ice. At the 1992 Super Bowl, Dorothy Hamill and Brian Boitano performed on ice made of the same plastic as grocery bags. Though it's tough enough for skate blades, the plastic ice isn't as slippery as natural ice.

STAR ••••••••••••••••

U.S. skater Michelle Kwan won the world title five times and the U.S. national title nine times. She seems to have been born to skate and drew all eyes to her with her remarkable grace under pressure. Even if she skated poorly during a competition, Kwan always seemed to roar back with enough spirit to win.

Michelle Kwan

THE ZAMBONI

What drives round and round the ice to keep it fresh and smooth for skaters? The Zamboni, of course! A Zamboni is like a huge razor blade on wheels with a built-in towel on the end. It gives the ice a close shave to resurface it and help stop it from chipping. Here's how it works.

1. The Shave

The big blade shaves the ice surface. How much ice does it cut off? It all depends—the rougher the ice, the more the blade shaves off.

2. Whisking Up the Shavings

A large screw collects the shavings, or snow, and feeds them into the snow tank at the front of the Zamboni. Later on, the shavings get dumped out.

3. Washing Up

The Zamboni has two water tanks. The wash-water tank flows to a squeegee-like conditioner behind the blade. This flushes dirt out of any deep cuts. The dirty wash water is vacuumed up and any leftover water is squeegeed off.

4. The Hot Towel Finish

A huge towel behind the conditioner spreads hot, clean water from the second water tank. The hot water softens any ruts or grooves in the ice and fills them in to make the surface smooth when the water freezes.

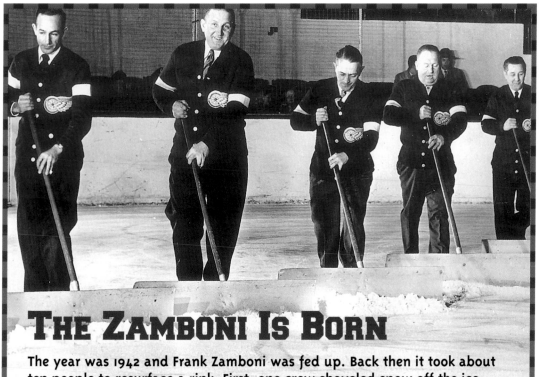

THE ZAMBONI IS BORN

The year was 1942 and Frank Zamboni was fed up. Back then it took about ten people to resurface a rink. First, one crew shoveled snow off the ice. Then another crew carried barrels of water to coat the ice with hot water. At best the job took an hour and a half—way too long for skaters to wait around. So he began building an ice-resurfacing machine in his backyard out of a Jeep and tires designed to grip the ice. Seven years and lots of tinkering later, Frank drove the first Zamboni into his California rink, Iceland, and smoothly resurfaced the ice in record time all by himself.

The Zamboni Hits the Bigtime

Around 1950, star figure skater Sonja Henie came to Frank Zamboni's rink to practice with her traveling show. After seeing his Zamboni in action, she asked Frank to build her one she could take on the road. He knew lots of people would see it at her shows and painted it fire-engine red. Once he was finished, he drove the Zamboni all the way to Chicago to deliver it to Sonja. Soon more orders rolled in and the cool machines began resurfacing rinks around the world.

Quick Answers to Slippery Questions

How fast does a Zamboni go?

Not very! The top speed of a Zamboni is about 14.5 km (9 mi.) per hour. That's about as fast as a slow tractor! At least it doesn't have far to go—each resurfacing job takes only about seven laps around a standard size rink.

Are Zambonis difficult to drive?

While you drive, you can barely see over the front, and there are twelve things to adjust. Plus, you have to get the job done between flights, or groups, of skaters!

Do Zambonis ever miss a spot?

Sure. Some Zamboni drivers call these gaps "vacations" or "holidays," depending on how big the gap is.

Skate Bite

In 2002, Zamboni driver Jimmy MacNeil took the Zamboni on its longest road trip ever. He drove one across Canada, from St. John's, Nfld., to Vancouver, B.C. His four-month "drive for gold" raised money for Canadian hockey programs.

LEGENDS ON ICE

Barbara Ann Scott

Beware! Bad Ice Ahead

The ice was far from perfect for the women's free skate at the 1948 Olympics in St. Moritz, Switzerland. Two hockey games earlier that day had gouged, dented, and dinged the outdoor ice from end to end. The weather was so mild that the crew couldn't flood the rink to fill in the holes and ruts without turning the ice into a pool of slush.

But difficult circumstances seemed to bring out the best in Canadian world champ Barbara Ann Scott. At the 1947 Worlds in Stockholm, Sweden, -20°C (-4°F) weather had made the outdoor rink as hard as cement. Nevertheless, Scott won the world title. "When you have to skate outside in the elements, you tend not to worry about the small stuff," she once said.

So when she and her coach arrived at the Olympic ice in 1948, they skated around to spot the worst ruts and holes. Then they adjusted her program, so she wouldn't do any jumps or spins over them. Once Scott stepped out on the rutted ice, she left all worries of holes and gouges behind. The graceful skater's dazzling jumps and spins won the free skate—and the gold medal.

Chapter 2

THESE BOOTS WERE MADE FOR SKATING

"Ouch! These boots are killing me." Chances are this very thought is running through the mind of at least one skater out there right now. Figure skaters wear skates as much as one-and-a-half to two sizes smaller than their shoes. In fact, many skaters can't bear to wear them for more than ten minutes if they're not skating.

What's more, elite skaters go through one or two pairs a year, and breaking in new boots is murder on the feet. The leather boots are so stiff and unbending that skaters can get cuts and scrapes on their ankles from new boots. It takes weeks for new boots to feel comfortable. And to top it all off, boots that don't fit properly can throw skaters off balance. Discover how skates have developed over time and how they can make or break a skater's performance.

Lace up and glide in! ➤

Check out how skates have slid forward over time to give figure skaters an edge on the ice.

3000 BCE

People in Scandinavia and Russia make the first skates using animal bones. They strap the bones on their feet and use long sticks like ski poles to glide on icy lakes.

1300s

Wooden skates that look like tiny skis are the rage, but they are clumsy and break easily. The Dutch change all that with new iron blades. The blades attach to a wood platform that is strapped on to shoes.

Around 1550

A Dutch blacksmith makes a mistake on a customer's order and forges thin metal skate blades with sharp edges. The new skates are faster and easier to control. Plus, the sharp edges actually grip the ice. For the first time, skaters can leave their poles behind. Skaters learn "the Dutch roll"—pushing off with one foot and gliding on the other—and modern skating is born.

1500s

1837

British skater Henry Boswell designs a skate for figure skaters. He shortens the front of the blade and lengthens the back for more stability and control. Boswell also adds a groove, or hollow, deepening the edges to help grip the ice better.

1848

American skater Edward Bushnell creates the first all-metal skates, making skates lighter and stronger.

1854

John Forbes of Dartmouth, N.S., designs a metal skate that doesn't need any straps. The skates lock on to shoes with adjustable clamps and a new craze grips North America.

1860s

New Yorker Jackson Haines screws blades right onto his street boots. This gives him enough stability to be able to perform his flashy new move—the sit spin. The move is impressive, but Haines' idea for permanent blades doesn't stick right away. Most people can't afford to buy a second pair of boots just for skating.

Jackson Haines

STICKS AND STONES, WE'LL SKATE ON BONES

- Ancient people made skates out of bones from elk, reindeer, and horses. Researchers have also found some ancient skates made from walrus tusks.
- Bone skates didn't have much "zoom, zoom." When researchers tried them out, they crawled along at 8 km (5 mi.) an hour. Talk about slow! Modern speed skaters zip around at up to 60 km (37 mi.) per hour.
- Bone skates didn't glide. In fact, ancient skaters greased the bones with animal lard to slide across the ice!

1890s

Pointy teeth like those of a saw appear on skate blades in Sweden. The teeth help skaters dig into the ice to jump, and the modern toe pick begins to take shape.

Early 1900s

Leather boots with permanent blades become standard skates. Skaters now have more stability for difficult moves.

Barbara Wagner and Robert Paul

Sonja Henie

1928

Around this time, Sonja Henie ditches the usual black boots for white ones. She will eventually win ten straight world titles and three Olympic gold medals. Women skaters everywhere copy the superstar and start lacing up in white boots.

1960s

For many years, boots have come to the calf. But as skaters' calf muscles flexed, the laces came loose. Bootmakers solve the problem by making low-cut boots. They also stiffen the ankle area to add more support when landing the new challenging jumps of the day.

2004

No limits! Figure skaters take to the air for more triples and quads than ever before. However, lots of injuries occur from the repeated landing in rigid boots. A hinged boot is designed that allows skaters to flex their ankles and ease the shock of landing.

THE NEXT GREAT SKATE?

Researchers are always designing new skates to try and reduce injuries caused by repeated jumping. So what's the next great skate? Will it be a hinged boot (see bottom left) that does the trick and catches on with skaters? One with elasticized leather? Or something else altogether? Only time will tell.

STAR • • • • • • • • • •

Canadian skater Gary Beacom is a rebel with applause. He does wild moves, such as a headstand on ice, and has wacky boots for any occasion—brown boots, neon boots, and even blue suede boots. The offbeat skater has even added handles to his boots to wear them on his hands and skate on all fours!

Gary Beacom

THE BOOTS AND BLADES

Most elite skaters have custom-made boots. Some boot makers even use a computer to make patterns for individual skaters. The final boots are stretched around wooden models, or lasts, of a skater's feet. Skaters then buy blades separately and have them mounted on the boots. Check out how the boots and blades help figure skaters strut their stuff.

Tongue Tied But Not Twisted

Figure skates have a wide tongue with rubber or sponge padding that allows skaters to flex their feet. Small round holes called eyelets and hooks lie beside the tongue. Skaters tie the laces tightly, so there's no slack between the eyelets or the hooks. That way, their skates and feet move as a unit for maximum control.

Fits Like a Glove

The boot is made of high quality elk or kangaroo leather. It fits snugly, so skaters can really feel the ice and have better foot control. That's why elite skaters wear boots in smaller sizes than their street shoes.

Wobble-Proof Ankles

The boots cover and support skaters' ankles. Boot makers use anywhere from one to four layers of leather, and even add extra stiffening material and ankle padding to produce a skate that has the correct support. The boots are so stiff, it's a little like wrapping a cast around your ankle!

A Real Heel

The first figure skates were blades strapped to a pair of street boots. Today, they're still made like old-fashioned boots with a stable heel to support the feet and ankles. A notch in the heel helps cut down stress on the Achilles tendon. Extra padding also helps guard against injury.

Pick a Toe Pick

Tiny sawlike teeth jut out at the front of the blade. Skaters plant these teeth into the ice to push off for certain jumps. Bigger toe picks can dig deep for a stronger push, but smaller picks won't catch the ice on spins.

They've Got Sole

Boot makers put a steel arch and other strengthening materials in the bottom of the boot to support the natural arches of skaters' feet. Then they attach a leather sole with cement.

Blades of Steel

The steel blades are only 4 mm (3/16 in.) thick. The blades have a groove, or "hollow," down the middle that creates sharp edges on each side. Ice dancers use blades that are shorter at the back. That way, they're less likely to step on a partner's blade when skating close together.

The Rocker

The blade's bottom has a rocker, or small curve. This helps skaters make turns on the ice. Some skaters feel a bigger rocker makes spins easier, because less of the blade contacts the ice.

Boot Up with Champions

Are skaters particular about their boots? You can bet your boots they are!

Hockey Skates to Go!

Four-time world champion Kurt Browning has been known to buy skates right off the rack and revamp them. He takes them to a skate shop and has leather cut away inside where it rubs against his feet and material added between the leather layers to stiffen them up. Sometimes, Browning even performs in hockey skates!

Lacing Up Luck

When Olympic champion Katarina Witt was competing, she always tied her skates three times for luck. She laced up the right one first, then the left, then she untied them and laced them up again—and again!

Break 'Em In Wetly

Olympic champion Brian Boitano breaks in new boots by filling them with hot water. Then he walks around in them for a week before he mounts the blades and takes to the ice.

A Sharpening Emergency

"Uh-oh!" thought Brian Boitano's skate sharpener just before the 1994 Olympics in Lillehammer, Norway. The sharpener had forgotten to make two of the usual number of passes to sharpen Boitano's blades. He knew Boitano would feel the difference and didn't want it to throw off Boitano's performance. So he hopped a plane to Lillehammer and made two more passes on each blade!

Skate Bite

In 1984, boot maker John Knebli played a joke on Brian Orser. Knebli sewed pieces of gold into a pair of boots he made for the Canadian champion and flatly refused to tell Orser where they were until he won the world title.

TIP

Look for skates that are snug but comfortable. Although elite skaters wear skates as many as two sizes smaller than their street shoes, that's not recommended for young skaters with growing feet. Try on a pair that's one size smaller than your shoes and see how they feel. When you're standing, you should be able to wiggle your toes but not lift your heel.

Quick Answers to Slippery Questions

Why do TV commentators always talk about skaters' edges?

Skaters do most of their moves on either the inside or outside edge of their blades. You can see the quality of skaters' "edges," or technique, by looking at the tracings they leave on the ice. Skating on a flat blade leaves two parallel lines on the ice—one from each edge. Skating on one edge leaves a single line.

How are blades sharpened?

A skate sharpener passes the blade over a diamond-tipped grinding wheel that spins very quickly. This hard tip deepens the "hollow" between the blade's edges. The deeper the hollow becomes, the sharper the blade feels to the skater.

How often do blades need sharpening?

Even though hockey players sharpen their blades for every game or even between periods, figure skaters do it only once a month. So a poor sharpening job can affect a skater's performance for quite a while! That's why elite skaters always go to the same sharpener. They want their blades sharpened the exact same way every time.

Barbara Underhill and Paul Martini

That Old Boot Magic

The Worlds were just three weeks away and Barbara Underhill had been struggling with new boots all season. First, an ankle injury kept her and partner Paul Martini out of the Canadian Championships. Then during their short program at the 1984 Olympics in Sarajevo, Yugoslavia, Underhill caught an edge and tumbled to the ice. The gold-medal hopefuls placed a sorry seventh.

Every move Underhill made on the ice felt unnatural—something just didn't feel right. Now their coach was asking the unlucky pair to call it quits so they wouldn't embarrass themselves at the Worlds. Underhill was devastated. She ran into fellow skater Brian Orser and began to cry. "Well, why don't you try last year's boots?" said Orser. "They worked last year."

It just so happened that the old boots were in the trunk of her car. Underhill ran and got them. Martini attached the old boots to her new blades. She laced them up and just like magic began whirling around the rink like her old self. The pair performed flawlessly at the Worlds and won the title. Underhill's old boots did the trick, and now they rest in the collection of artifacts at Canada's Sports Hall of Fame.

Chapter 3

INVENTIVE MOVES

Whee! Oh, what fun it is to glide on two way-cool metal blades! Soon after people strapped animal bones on their feet to cross frozen lakes, they began to skate just for fun. Early skaters delighted in the trail-like tracings their blades left on the ice. They began moving in patterns that cut circles, figure eights, and even hearts into the ice. The sport of figure skating was born. But not all figure skaters were content to leave it at that. They took a hop, spin, and a jump from there, inventing breathtaking moves that put the thrills and spills into the sport that the world knows and loves today. Turn the page to travel back in time and discover the twists and turns of these rebellious inventors of the ice.

Qing Pang and
Jian Tong

Go figure!

HOW THE ICE WAS WON

Trace the footsteps of early figure skaters and see how they tamed the slippery ice to carve out a path for the sport.

IT FIGURES

The name "figure skating" goes back to the 1700s, when the world's first figure skating club sprung up in Edinburgh, Scotland. Back then, the object was to carve figures, such as the numbers eight or six, on the ice with your blades. Anyone who wanted to join the club had to pass a test that included carving circles with each foot. Club skaters also traced figures called the "wild goose" and the "worm," where a group of skaters followed a leader's curves on the ice. In early competitions, skaters did compulsory, or school, figures—forty-one figures based on the number eight. They also traced a special figure of their own design. Judges marked their performances by peering at the tracings left on the ice. Eventually, competitors had to trace each figure three times in the same spot. A perfect performance left only one line on the ice.

LONE SKATER "BREAKS THE ICE"

In 1902, Madge Syers went where no woman had gone before—into the World Championships. There was no actual rule barring women because no one dreamed they would ever enter! Officials let Syers compete, and the bold English skater stunned the world. She won the silver medal and skated circles around the men—so much so that the gold medal winner Ulrich Salchow even gave her his medal. But the International Skating Union (ISU) wasn't impressed. They banned women with the flimsy excuse that their long skirts hid their feet from the judges. Syers was undeterred and simply shortened her skirts. The next year England held a competition open to both men and women and wouldn't you know, Syers won! In 1906, the ISU finally caved in and started a female competition. Finally, an event that women could call their own.

Madge and Edgar Syers

How can you trace a figure eight on the ice?
Try this experiment and see.

1 Find a clear patch of ice so you can see the lines carved by your skates.

2 Push off with your left foot and glide on the outside edge of the right.

DARING PAIR TAKES TO THE AIR

Once Syers broke the ice for women, pair skating took off. But the pairs did not—their skates remained on the ice at all times. There were no flashy lifts, where the man hoists the woman overhead, or throw

Andrée Joly and Pierre Brunet

jumps, where the man hurls the woman spinning through the air. Pair skaters waltzed around the rink as if it were a ballroom. Even side-by-side moves were rare until the 1924 Olympics in Chamonix, France, where Andrée Joly and Pierre Brunet let go of one another's hands and took to the air with shocking flair. The innovative French champions did more side-by-side moves and spins than any pair before them. What's more, they used never-before-seen lifts and separate jumps. Their performance thrilled spectators. Some judges gave them high marks, but others gave them really low marks for their "circus tricks." Joly and Brunet left with only the bronze, but their daring moves soon set a new standard for pairs everywhere.

TV WIPES OUT FIGURES

Fans were shocked by the women's free skate broadcast from the 1972 Olympics at Sapporo, Japan. Beatrix Schuba of Austria won the gold medal, Karen Magnussen of Canada the silver, and Janet Lynn of the U.S. the bronze. But both Magnussen and Lynn had beaten Schuba hands, er, skates down in the free skate. How could this be? Well, what the fans hadn't seen on TV was the part of the competition where they skated figures. Not only had Schuba placed first in figures, but figures counted for 60 percent of the skaters' scores. Schuba only needed an average free skate to win gold. Even the ISU felt something had to be done. Figures were the ultimate test of skill, but they were just plain boring to watch on TV. So the ISU reworked the scoring system and lowered how much figures counted until, in 1990, they were eliminated altogether! However, not everyone was pleased. Some say figures remain the heart of all skating technique.

Magnussen, Schuba, and Lynn

3 Keep gliding in the path of a circle until you return to the point where you started.

4 Now push off with the right foot and glide on the outside edge of the left.

5 Keep gliding in the path of a circle until you return to the starting point.

6 Look at the tracing you made on the ice. What do you notice?

Answer on page 64.

DARING MOVES THROUGH TIME

Just how did figure skating change over the years? Check out this timeline of bold moves made by the sport's rebels and inventors.

Late 1700s

1, 2, 3…jump. Figure skating's first official jump: a hop over hats! One of the requirements for new members to join the Edinburgh Skating Club in Scotland is to jump over a pile of stacked hats—first one hat, then two, and finally three. Wowee!

1860s

He skates to music? With dance moves? How horrifying! Jackson Haines offends the skating elite with an unprecented program in which he skates across the entire rink. The American also invents the sit spin—legend says he spent nine years perfecting it! These rebel moves eventually become the heart of modern figure skating.

1882

Norwegian dynamo Axel Paulsen figure skates as well as he speed skates. He skates forward, jumps into the air, completes one-and-a-half turns and lands skating backward. Paulsen even does the never-before-seen jump in speed skates! The axel is born. It remains the most difficult jump.

Around 1910

World champ Ulrich Salchow of Sweden invents a new jump. He takes off on the back inside edge of one foot and lands on the back outside edge of the other foot. And so the salchow takes flight.

Ulrich Salchow

1920

U.S. champion Theresa Weld lands a salchow at the Olympics, the first full-turn jump by a woman. Instead of extra marks, the judges scold her for "unfeminine" behavior. Weld ends up with the bronze, but women start to add jumps to their programs anyway.

1920s

Swedish Olympic champ Gillis Grafstrom constantly experiments with new moves. He creates the change sit spin, in which he changes legs in mid spin, and the flying sit spin, in which he jumps into the spin. How's that for a new spin on things?

1928

Sixteen-year-old Sonja Henie combines ballet routines with athletic jumps and spins. The Norwegian's revolutionary free skate lights up the ice like none before. Henie wins Olympic gold and sets a new path.

1930s

Austrian skater Alois Lutz lifts one foot, looks over the opposite shoulder, and jumps into a full rotation. The result? The lutz jump—what else?!

1947

U.S. champion Dick Button jumps into a camel spin at the Worlds. This move becomes the flying camel. At the time, people call it the "Button camel."

1948

Rehearsing for the free skate at the Olympics, Button lands the world's first double axel jump. No one dreams he will risk the new jump in the competition, but Button does and lands cleanly. Phew!

Dafoe and Bowden

Donald Jackson

1950s

Canadian pair champs Frances Dafoe and Norris Bowden pull off the world's first throw jump, catch lift, twist lift, and overhead lasso lift, in which the man lifts the woman and twirls her around like a lasso!

1962

Donald Jackson lands the world's first triple lutz jump. The Canadian champion receives a record-setting set of seven perfect marks for his landmark performance.

What's a head-banger?

An illegal pairs' move guaranteed to make you catch your breath. The man lifts the woman overhead then drops her to one side headfirst, so her head almost touches the ice. Then he swings her all the way around until she's upright beside him.

What's "doing a Midori"?

Jumping into or over the boards at the side of the rink. It gets its name from Japan's Midori Ito. At the 1991 Worlds, Ito skated so close to the boards that she jumped out of the rink into a camera pit!

What's a flutz?

When a skater changes a lutz jump into a flip jump just seconds before takeoff. There's no rule against flutzing like this. But a flip jump is easier than a lutz, so skaters may lose marks.

Bourne and Kraatz

1994

People cannot take their eyes off Canadian ice dancing champs Shae-Lynn Bourne and Victor Kraatz as they hydroblade at the Olympics. The pair lean out low, almost parallel to the ice on one blade. Even their practice sessions are mesmerizing!

Miki Ando

1976

Terry Kubicka flips out at the Worlds. The U.S. champ does a backflip, somersaulting backward in midair. The ISU bans the move overnight, saying it's too dangerous.

Late 1970s

Swiss champion Denise Biellmann lifts one leg behind her, grabs the foot with both hands, stretches the leg up overhead, and spins around like a top. And with that the biellmann spin whirls into the world.

1988

Kurt Browning busts out at the Worlds. The Canadian champ completes a quadruple toe loop—the world's first quadruple jump.

2002

Miki Ando of Japan shakes up the competition at the Junior Grand Prix final by completing a quadruple salchow—the first quad jump by a female skater.

STARS

In the 1990s, this pair could pull off a daring lift like no other. Eisler threw Brasseur high above his head. Then Brasseur, who looked as if she were lying down in midair, made three complete turns as she fell toward Eisler's head. He caught her just before she was about to crash into his noggin!

Isabelle Brasseur and Lloyd Eisler

What's figure skating's next move? Will it be a quintuple loop or axel? Never say it can't be done...

LEGENDS ON ICE

Dick Button

Mission Impossible

In 1952, triple jumps didn't exist. Many said they were impossible. But Richard "Dick" Button was a skater on a mission: triple loop or bust. And bust he did. Not only did he miss the triple completely, he started to have problems with all his jumps. So Button stopped working on the triple entirely.

Then one day he tried the triple loop on a lark. He got it and didn't let go. Just before the Olympics, he landed the triple loop in front of an audience for the first time. But the day before the Olympic free skate, Button tried the jump and fell. Everyone wondered if he would play it safe in the competition—everyone but Button, that is.

Partway through his Olympic free skate, he jumped up and nailed his prized triple loop perfectly! It was the first triple landed in a competition. The crowd roared like thunder and the judges' marks did not disappoint. Button grabbed the gold medal, and skating jumps were never the same. Mission accomplished!

Chapter 4

THE SCIENCE OF EXPLOSIVE MOVES

Scratch! Scratch! Most spins are quiet, but not the scratch spin. It requires the skater to balance near the front of her skate blade and this makes her toe pick scratch the ice as she spins. This upright spin also allows her to spin with incredible speed. "Ooh!" Onlookers gasp as she turns into a blur.

"Aah!" The crowd catches its breath as a skater jumps and whirls through the air. Will he land cleanly without a wobble, or tumble to the ice? Jumps are the most difficult and riskiest moves the skater can attempt. After all, there's just no way to disguise a fall. On the other hand, executing a jump cleanly scores points with the judges and causes fans to go wild. Check out the science of jumps and spins—a skater's most explosive tricks on ice.

Spin this way!

JUST SPINNING AROUND

Want to know how skaters become a "human blur"? At speeds of up to 160 kph (100 mph), the scratch spin is the fastest on ice! Skaters often end their program with one for an exciting finish.

CONTROLLING THE FORCE

Notice how the skater's skirt flares up and away from her body? Objects moving quickly in a circle are affected by an invisible physical force called centrifugal force. This force also pulls the skater's arms and legs up and away. The skater must use all her strength to hold them in close to her body.

1 PREPARING TO SPIN

The skater enters the scratch spin by taking a big step forward with her left foot. She steps with a bent left knee onto the outside edge of her left foot. Then the skater turns and shifts her balance to the inside edge.

2 SWING TO BEGIN

Holding her arms out to the sides, she swings her free leg forward to start momentum for the spin. She balances on the ball of her skating foot and traces small circles backward on the spot. This centers the spin on the ice.

3 PICKING UP SPEED

The skater slowly straightens her skating leg to make the circles smaller. To start spinning faster, she brings her free foot toward her skating knee and clasps her arms in front as if she were hugging a tree trunk.

4 TO THE MAX

To spin even faster, the skater pulls her free foot down heel first and crosses it over the skating foot. She pulls her arms in and up overhead. Finally, she presses her legs together and tightens her stomach and buttock muscles.

SPOT THE SPIN

Take a good look at these photos of figure skaters doing spins.
Can you match up each photo with the correct name of the spin?

A. Sit spin
B. Layback spin
C. Pancake spin

Answer on page 64.

Do spins make them dizzy?

Yep! Although a few get used to the feeling, even some top skaters say they get dizzy with every spin. They must try to cope with the dizziness after the spin. Some skaters focus on a spot in the crowd, boards, or ice until they feel better. Skaters learn not to plan performing a jump right after a spin!

What's a death drop?

No, skaters don't drop dead when they blow a jump! A death drop combines a flying sit spin and a flying camel spin (see page 24). Skaters take off for a flying sit spin, drop into a brief flying camel, and then drop down into a sit spin. It looks deadly because a skater's body splays flat out in the air parallel to the ice briefly before dropping into the camel spin.

TRY THIS!

1 Sit in the swivel chair. Have lots of open space around it.

2 Hold your arms straight out to the sides and start spinning. If you feel dizzy or sick, just stop spinning.

3 Bring your arms in and cross them over your chest, like skaters do as they spin. What do you notice?

4 Stop spinning by holding your arms and legs out.

Answer on page 64.

You don't have to figure skate to check out the dizzy science of spinning.

Try this experiment and see.

YOU WILL NEED

• a swivel chair

Spinning Tops

• A top skater can complete up to six full turns a second and seventy turns in one spin.

• American Ronald Robertson spun a record 240 turns in a minute. He could even spin faster than an electric fan!

• Swiss skater Nathalie Krieg set a record with a three-minute-and-twenty-second spin.

THE THROW JUMP

I s any move more explosive or dangerous in figure skating than a pair's throw jump? Not likely! In a throw axel, the man flings the woman upward and outward. She flies through the air higher, faster, and longer than any singles skater. What's more, the boost from her partner may completely throw off the landing. Check out a throw triple axel in action and see for yourself how thrilling it is.

1 The skaters glide backward, hip to hip, to setup for takeoff.

2 The man curls his right arm around the woman's back.

3 The pair turn forward.

4 The woman pushes onto the outside edge of her left foot.

5 As the woman takes off, she kicks her right leg up and the man springs up by straightening his legs, giving her a boost into the air.

6 The woman flies up.

7 She rotates three and a half times in the air...

8 ...traveling quite far away from her partner.

9 The woman lands skating backwards on the outside edge of her right foot.

10 The partners skate back to each other.

THE DEATH SPIRAL

Hold my hand and don't let go! It takes guts to spiral around your partner with your head almost touching the ice. Check out the death spiral, a pairs move that's only slightly less scary and daring than its name.

1 The pair enters a death spiral holding hands. The man skates backward and the woman skates forward.

2 Skating on the inside edge of the right foot, the woman bends her right knee. She leans over sideways toward the man's feet as he pulls her forward.

3 He plants his left toe pick firmly in the ice. The woman leans back parallel to the ice. Her inside edge and her partner's hand are her only support!

4 The man spins around his left toe as the woman spirals on her right foot's inside edge. The pair must do at least one full rotation.

5 The woman arches her back until the man lifts her up to exit from the spiral.

A Perfect Match

Pairs skating isn't easy. Not only do skaters have to jump and spin like singles skaters, but they must perform moves in unison, or at exactly the same time. If either skater is a little off, the team loses marks. Experts say it's an advantage if the woman is small and light and the man is big and strong like 1988 and 1994 Olympic champions Ekaterina Gordeeva and Sergei Grinkov of Russia. But it's not absolutely necessary. It may look like the man is doing all the work in pair lifts and throws, but the woman actually provides the spring, or momentum. Great pairs not only respect and trust each other, they have an inexplicable chemistry like Gordeeva and Grinkov that makes them seem to skate as one.

Ekaterina Gordeeva and Sergei Grinkov

31

THE QUAD

Kurt Browning rocked the 1988 Worlds when he spun four times in the air and touched down for a solid landing. No one had landed a quadruple toe loop jump in competition before—or any other "quad" for that matter. Even today, the move is risky. Experts say it's no accident that the first successful quad was a toe loop. It's the easiest jump for most skaters and its toe-pick takeoff hoists skaters high into the air. Check it out!

IT'S A LUTZ, IT'S A LOOP, IT'S A TRIPLE FLIP!

How can you tell which jump is which without flipping out? Skaters do six main jumps in competition but all the jumps look the same in the air. They even land all the jumps the same—on the outside edge of the right foot gliding backward. But with this handy checklist, you'll be able to tell which jump is which.

THE AXEL	THE FLIP	THE LUTZ
Takeoff Edge: Outside	*Takeoff Edge:* Inside	*Takeoff Edge:* Outside
Toe-pick Boost?: No	*Toe-pick Boost?:* Yes	*Toe-pick Boost?:* Yes
Landing Foot: Opposite from takeoff foot	*Landing Foot:* Opposite from takeoff foot	*Landing Foot:* Opposite from takeoff foot
Telltale Sign: Skating forward to take off. Skaters take off for all other jumps while skating backward.	*Telltale Sign:* A quick liftoff. Skaters turn backward, get a quick toe-pick boost, and then take off lickety-split.	*Telltale Sign:* A long, glide toward a corner of the rink. Skaters skate backward, and then glide to take off.

1 **2** **3** **4** **5**

PREPARING TO JUMP

The skater glides backward on the outside edge of his right foot with his knee bent and his left leg extended straight back (1).

TAKING OFF

The skater jabs his left toe into the ice as he springs off his right foot (2). The toe pick acts like a pole vaulter's pole and lifts him into the air. The skater spins to his left and pulls his arms to his chest to spin faster.

FLYING AROUND AND AROUND

The skater crosses his left foot over his right, points his toes, and squeezes his legs together. This also helps him spin around faster. He rotates one (3), two (4), three (5), and finally four (6) times in the air.

THE LOOP

Takeoff Edge: Outside

Toe-pick Boost?: No

Landing Foot: Same as takeoff foot

Telltale Sign: Taking off without the toe pick and then landing on the same foot.

THE SALCHOW

Takeoff Edge: Inside

Toe-pick Boost?: No

Landing Foot: Opposite from takeoff foot

Telltale Sign: Gliding backward, then moving the free leg and arms out and quickly back in.

THE TOE LOOP

Takeoff Edge: Outside

Toe-pick Boost?: Yes

Landing Foot: Same as takeoff foot

Telltale Sign: Taking off with a toe-pick boost and then landing on the same foot.

LANDING ON ONE FOOT

As the skater comes back down, he opens his arms to slow his spin. He lands on his right outside edge and bends his right knee to cushion the landing (7). He glides backward and lifts his left leg back and up (8). Ta da!

What makes the axel so tough?

The axel is the only jump in which skaters move forward to take off. Skaters also take off from one foot and land on the other backward. That means they must turn one more half rotation than for other jumps.

Does a triple jump take longer than a double?

Nope. Skaters spend the same time in the air for each. They use more energy to jump higher for a triple axel than a double. They also hold their arms and legs closer to their body so that they spin faster.

What's a triple-triple?

Whoosh! Click! Whoosh! A triple-triple is a combination jump in which skaters take off for one triple jump, land, and immediately take off for another triple.

Why do skaters often fall apart on combination jumps?

Combinations are tough because skaters can't step or turn between the jumps. They must take off for the second jump from the same edge on which they land the first jump. That's why you can bet the second jump in a combination will be a loop or toe loop. Since skaters always land on the outside edge skating backward and can't step or turn, they have no choice!

Timothy Goebel

The Quad King

No one ever had to prod American Timothy Goebel for a quad. He began practicing them when he was just fourteen. As a junior, he landed the first quad salchow in competition. In 1999, he became the first skater to land three quads in one program. He was even working on a quad-quad combination. People took to calling him the Quad King.

"This is an Olympic sport, not Olympic art," he once said. "To keep improving the sport, you need new tricks." But the judges disagreed. At the 2002 Olympics, where he again landed an incredible three quads in one program, he won only the bronze. The elegant Russians Alexei Yagudin (with two quads) and Evgeni Plushenko (with only one quad) won gold and silver.

But that didn't stop the Quad King from trying to outjump the rest of the world. In 2003, he even attempted to land an amazing four quads in one program. "I just want to do something different," he said at the time. Even though this human jumping bean didn't pull it off, Timothy raised the standards of jumping higher than ever before.

Chapter 5

THE COMPLETE ATHLETE

Whew! Don't let anybody tell you that figure skaters aren't athletes. Skating a long program is like running a 100-metre dash and a long distance race all at once. Sound crazy? Well, a sprinter exerts a quick burst of energy to run 100 metres in ten seconds or less. Likewise, a skater exerts an explosive blast of energy to do a triple jump or a quad in a second flat.

But the skater doesn't stop there. Like a long-distance runner, the skater keeps going for a full four minutes or more. All this time, the skater is executing demanding sequences of footwork, jumps, and spins. No wonder figure skaters need strength, speed, stamina, and endurance. Get the scoop on how competitive skaters whip their bodies and minds into tip-top condition.

Shape up!

THE BODY

You're an elite skater performing for your country at the Olympic Games. You're the last to skate, and you've got a shot at the gold medal. At the end of an exhausting program, do you have enough energy left to do another triple and grab the gold? You bet you do! Thanks to your off-ice training program, you're in peak physical condition.

You've been training off the ice all year long to increase your strength, flexibility, and endurance—the ability to go all out without letting up. You've been lifting weights, but not to bulk up like the Incredible Hulk. Bulking up not only slows down your speed of rotation during spins and jumps, it also looks bad on figure skaters. Instead, you've been pumping iron to strengthen your entire body so you can jump higher with more control.

You've also been doing power, or plyometric, training. Now you can explode in and out of jumps faster. You'll need that burst of power during a quad to squeeze in an extra rotation before you land. Plyometric drills, such as jumping on the spot, doing long jumps, and jumping on and off a box, have helped to increase the power of your ankles, knees, hips, torso, and shoulders.

You've been cycling, running, or swimming to build up your endurance. If you didn't, you'd be feeling pretty tired near the end of your program. Your body needs oxygen for energy, but as you're skating, sometimes you can't get that energy fast enough. Endurance exercises train your body to make the energy you need without oxygen. That way you can go all out and bust that last triple to grab first place from your rivals.

Skaters Just Gotta Dance

Step, plié, step! In the early 1900s, young Sonja Henie studied ballet with the teacher of the famous Russian ballerina Anna Pavlova. Henie brought the grace, artistry, and fluid movements she learned in ballet into skating and radically changed the sport. At ten, Sonja became Norway's national skating champion and at fifteen she won her first of three Olympic gold medals. Since then, many skaters have included ballet in their training. Not only does ballet help them move more gracefully and fluidly on the ice, but it can also increase their power to jump high and strengthen their lower back for more control. Many ice dancers also take ballroom dance classes to learn the real steps before they transform them for the ice. You might say skaters just gotta dance to enhance their performance.

Anna Pavlova

STAR

Sasha Cohen, 2006 Olympic silver medalist and U.S. champion, includes ballet and yoga in her off-ice training. "Yoga makes me a much stronger athlete," she once said. "It's a great way to get warmed up and tone all my muscles and keep my whole body strong." Sometimes, Sasha even incorporates yoga poses into her moves on the ice.

Sasha Cohen

Fuel Up

You can't jump, spin, or even skate on an empty tank. Your body needs fuel. That doesn't mean you should eat like there's no tomorrow. Lugging extra weight around can affect your balance and timing. But you don't want to starve yourself either. A well-balanced diet gives you the energy you need to skate competitively and helps strengthen your body to prevent injuries.

Top skaters need to fuel up on carbohydrates, fats, and proteins from each of the four food groups—grains, meats and meat substitutes, fruits and vegetables, and dairy—in the following proportions:

55 to 75% of your diet—carbohydrates: Eating fruit, vegetables, and whole-grain breads, cereals and pasta, gives skaters their number one source of energy.

25 to 35% of your diet—fats: Eating cheese, yogurt, peanut butter, and dressing on a salad gives skaters energy they can use and store.

12 to 15% of your diet—proteins: Eating chicken, beef, fish, milk, tofu, and eggs helps build up muscles and repair body tissues.

WHAT'S UP, DOC?

Skaters are jumping higher and more often than ever. The more they train, the more they gain, but also strain. About half of skating injuries are due to strain on joints and muscles.

RUNAWAY TRAINING

It's not easy getting to the top. When Olympic champion Tara Lipinski was fourteen, she got up at 7:15 a.m., headed to the rink, and skated for two and a half hours. After having lunch, she skated for another hour and a half, and went home for school from 3:00 p.m. to 7:00 p.m. Then she ate dinner, did homework, unwound with a bit of TV, and fell into bed. The next day, she did it all over again! Competitive skaters train six days a week for as many as four hours a day on the ice and three hours off it. Training runs their lives. Some figure skaters even move to a new city to train with a particular coach.

JUMP CRASH JUMP

Jumps are tough to learn. Beginning skaters may fall more than ten or twenty times a lesson learning jumps. Some even wear crash pads under their clothes to cushion their hips and tailbone. Next, they begin to learn doubles and then triples. Even after they learn these jumps, skaters must repeat them over and over to perform them well. Top skaters do anywhere from fifty to one hundred jumps a day. Repeating moves like this can lead to overuse injuries, such as tendonitis (see right) and stress fractures.

Michelle Kwan

STRAINING TO GAIN IS A PAIN

Up, up, and…POP goes the muscle! Ouch. Sometimes, exploding into a jump puts so much pressure on a muscle that it overstretches or tears. Muscle strains in the hips, which skaters flex to jump, often happen to skaters who bang out triples and quads. These injuries are known as groin strains and they can knock skaters right out of competition. At the 2006 Olympics, for example, Michelle Kwan did a triple flip that didn't feel right as she was practicing. She left in pain. That night a doctor's diagnosis revealed a severe groin strain. The doctor said it was impossible for her to jump, land, and skate without risk of serious injury. The groin strain forced Michelle to withdraw from the Olympics, shattering her lifelong dream of winning a gold medal.

What-the-itis?

Tendonitis from overusing knee and ankle joints, the lower back, or hips is common among figure skaters. Tendons are flexible cords inside the body that attach muscles to bones. When a tendon is used too much, it can swell up and cause pain, tenderness, or stiffness. Jumper's knee affects the tendon that attaches the thigh muscles to the kneecap and the shinbone. At first, skaters may feel jumper's knee as pain just below the kneecap after a training session. But if left untreated, the pain gradually becomes worse and skaters may have to stop jumping altogether to get treatment and recover.

Tendonitis can also make skaters' bones susceptible to stress fractures. These are tiny cracks that develop in areas that undergo repeated stress, such as a skater's takeoff leg for toe-pick jumps.

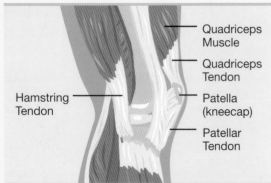

Quadriceps Muscle

Quadriceps Tendon

Hamstring Tendon

Patella (kneecap)

Patellar Tendon

Coaches with the Mostest

A great figure skating coach is someone you can understand and with whom you can communicate. A coach's main job is to help you work on the techniques of skating, jumping, and spinning. So you want to find someone who you can really learn from. At the beginning of the competitive season, your coach will plan each of your lessons to work on the techniques and skills you need to master to achieve your goals. A coach with the mostest will help you develop a mental edge, too. The coach also learns how to read you like a book, knowing when to push you and when to give you a break.

Quick Answers to Slippery Questions

Does practice make jumps perfect?

Nope. A skater can have a so-so day. Before she even knows it, she might blow it and fall on a jump she can usually do in her sleep. But practice does make jumps as good as they get.

What's lace bite?

Sometimes, the tongue of a skater's boot can bite, or irritate, the skater's shin. Luckily, lace bite has a few simple remedies, such as positioning the tongue correctly, lacing up differently, or adding padding between the tongue and the shin.

What are pump bumps?

"Check out the bumps on the back of her heels!" Pump bumps develop when boots are too big for a skater's feet and her heels slip up and down, rubbing against the interior of the boots.

TIP

Warming up and stretching before you practice can help prepare your body for the shock of falling. Warm up by jumping rope or jogging on the spot for five to eight minutes. Then do ten to fifteen minutes of light stretches for your whole body.

STAR

Yu-Na Kim has a huge flock of coaches. The South Korean moved to Toronto to work with a specific spin coach, jump coach, and skating coach. And then there's her personal trainer and a choreographer, too! Maybe they should all wear shirts that say "Team Yu-Na."

Yu-Na Kim

THE MIND

Experts say that once athletes are at the Olympic level of competition, their physical abilities are usually very similar. So it's the athlete that has the mental edge that wins. Find out how the mind can make or break a performance.

TALKING TO YOURSELF

You are skating your long program at the Olympics. You fly into the air for a triple toe loop. Something doesn't feel right and you touch the ice with one hand as you land. "Great. Just great. There goes the gold medal…" you say to yourself. But hold on. Get down on yourself like that, and your whole routine could go downhill in a heartbeat. Several studies show that athletes' self-talk—things they say to themselves as they perform—influences their success.

SAY WHAT?

Researchers think that negative self-talk can lead to poor performances, while positive self-talk can give athletes the chance to perform well. So always focus on what you did right—like staying on your landing foot instead of falling on your derrière. Tell yourself positive things such as: "I hung on for the landing. I can do this." But don't expect positive self-talk to change things overnight. To keep a strong mental edge, you need to practice positive self-talk just like you practice jumps.

VISUALIZE YOURSELF, DUDE!

Want to nail a quad under pressure? Visualize mental pictures, or even a movie, of yourself completing all the moves of a quadruple jump during a packed competition. Some figure skaters learn skills, rehearse moves, and see success through this technique of visualization. The idea is that as you see mental pictures of yourself doing jumps and spins, they take root in your mind. Then, when you're skating in a competition you instinctively execute the jump or spin successfully. Studies show that visualization improves athletes' performances. When one group of athletes gets only physical training and another gets both physical and visualization training, the second group outperforms the first. But visualization is not a sure-fire way to success. Scientists don't understand why it works for some athletes and not for others.

NICE JOB ON THE LUTZ, YOU NAILED IT!!

THANKS, AND YOU REALLY PULLED OFF THAT CAMEL.

The Olympic Mind Games

No competition plays on skaters' minds with as much pressure as the Olympics—and pressure is all in the mind. When you feel under pressure, you may not deliver your best performance. Just ask Canadian skating dynamo Kurt Browning. The four-time world champion competed in the Olympics three times without winning a single medal. Check out some of his thoughts and feelings at play before, during, and after his performances.

Kurt Browning

1 1988 Calgary

The Olympics are in Kurt's hometown. He feels so much pressure that he can barely breathe and bawls his eyes out at practice. "You're okay," says his coach. "No, I'm not okay," says Kurt. "I'm scared like you wouldn't believe." He finishes eighth.

3 1994 Lillehammer: the Short Program

Kurt loses an edge and falls on a triple flip—a jump he hasn't had trouble with for years. He starts thinking about Albertville and does a single axel instead of the required double.

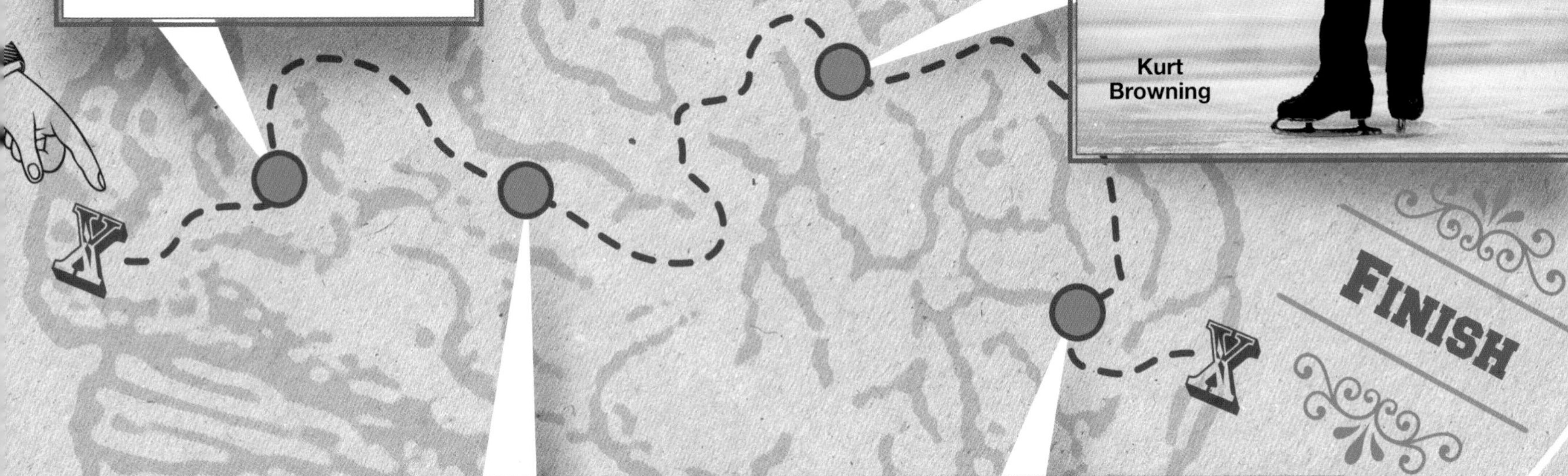

2 1992 Albertville

Having won the last three Worlds, Kurt's the heavy favorite for the gold medal. He feels frustrated at every practice. He thinks the ice is in terrible condition and finishes sixth. "I was so not myself," he says later.

4 1994 Lillehammer: the Long Program

The botched short program leaves Kurt in twelfth place in his last Olympics. With a medal out of reach, he thinks he has no choice but to go out strong. Kurt skates so beautifully that he brings the house down and rises up to fifth place!

FINISH

41

Elvis Stojko

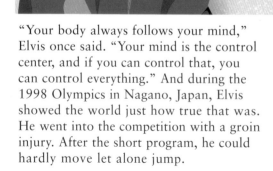

POW!!

The Man Was Kung Fu Skating

Ballet moves didn't cut it for Elvis Stojko. The three-time Canadian world champ was a black belt in karate and he pumped up his programs with kung fu moves and music from martial arts movies. The judges were not impressed and often gave him artistic marks much lower than his marks for technical merit.

But Elvis refused to change. In fact, the intense focus and body control he had learned in martial arts became the key to his skating success. Elvis was the first skater to land quads consistently and to perform them in combination with other jumps. His amazing ability to focus allowed him to shut out all distractions during competitions. Other skaters called him the Terminator.

"Your body always follows your mind," Elvis once said. "Your mind is the control center, and if you can control that, you can control everything." And during the 1998 Olympics in Nagano, Japan, Elvis showed the world just how true that was. He went into the competition with a groin injury. After the short program, he could hardly move let alone jump.

Still, he performed his long program, landing eight triples bang-on. When he was done, Elvis barely made it off the ice. His gutsy performance won the silver medal and Canada's Meritorious Service Cross for "tremendous courage under such adversity." Like the Terminator, Elvis proved he was made of true metal, er, mettle.

Chapter 6

BREATHTAKING PERFORMANCES

Click... Sometimes everything seems to fall into place and—gasp!—a skater delivers a program that takes your breath away. "Wow! That was awesome!" you blurt out. Chances are it was more than a clean performance of required jumps and spins that moved you. Nowadays, skaters need what experts call "the whole package" to really touch an audience.

This whole package is a program of stellar jumps and spins—a.k.a. the technical elements—executed with great flair—a.k.a. the artistic presentation—to music. A good program brings out a skater's personality—from the playful and humorous side to the deep and moody.

Nowadays, many elite skaters work with a choreographer to interpret the music and plan each and every movement, gesture, and facial expression they make during their program. But that wasn't always so. Discover what sparked the trend to work with choreographers and how costumes have evolved to suit skaters' programs perfectly.

Valerie Marcoux
and Craig Buntin

Go behind the scenes

PUTTING A PROGRAM TOGETHER

Help! We've got a battle to win! At the 1987 Worlds, Brian Orser beat rival Brian Boitano soundly with superior artistry. In just eleven months, the two Brians were set to clash again at the 1988 Olympics in Calgary, Canada. So Boitano's coach called choreographer Sandra Bezic for help with his program.

Brian Boitano

JUMPS AREN'T EVERYTHING

Boitano had the jumps—some people say he was the best jumper the sport has ever seen. But in 1987, even he admitted he was like a "technical robot" on the ice. His programs lacked artistry and emotion. In fact, when Bezic saw Boitano skate at the Worlds, she noticed that he looked uncomfortable when he tried to smile at the audience.

DO WHAT WORKS FOR YOU

But Bezic also noticed Boitano's "precise technique" and "physical power." At 1.8 m (5 ft. 11 in.), he was taller than his rivals. Bezic thought the small, quick moves in his programs worked against the big skater. She suggested they play up his size and strength by focusing on simple but majestic moves. One of these was a long, slow spread eagle, in which he glided on a curve with his heels facing each other. Audiences gasped as Boitano sailed all the way around in a circle, and the spread eagle became one of his signature moves.

AN "ICE TUNES" MIX

But what's a long program without music? Bezic suggested the theme from the movie *Napoleon*. As soon as Boitano heard the military-style music he knew it was for him. So they began editing—taking a bit from here and a bit from there—to create an inspiring soundtrack for his program. Skaters usually do their most difficult jump early in the program, when they're most fresh. Boitano wanted to open with a 'tano lutz, his own lutz variation in which he jumped with one arm up to the sky, then a triple axel combination. Bezic made edits to the music to match the steps he took between the jumps.

A STORY ON ICE

Part of choreography is making a "story" to inspire the skater's movements. Even if the audience never gets the exact story, it gives the skater a character and emotions to express through every move. Bezic's idea was for Boitano to portray a five-part story of a soldier: marching to war, having doubts after battle, dancing at a ball, showing his true self beneath the uniform, and then a victory march. They also outfitted Boitano in a costume of a soldier's uniform. As it turned out, Brian Orser's program had a military theme, too. No wonder their Olympic showdown was billed the "Battle of the Brians!"

JAMMIN' AND PLANNIN'

Once the music was chosen, Bezic and Boitano hit the ice to "jam"—playing around with moves and gestures. First, she did a step then he mirrored it. Step by step, move by move, the program began to come together. Bezic placed moves where they'd look best from the judges' point of view, and built time in the program for Boitano to recover from a jump before taking off for another jump. She also tried to have him cover as much ice as possible so that he wasn't doing all his best moves in the same spot.

PRACTICE MAKES PERFECT

Boitano ran through the program over and over, just like he would at a competition. He didn't stop or pause when he made mistakes, he just practiced those bits again afterward. And the hard work paid off. Boitano's new program blew people away. Gone was the robot jumper. In his place, skated a dynamic young man whose emotions reached out and touched the audience. Bezic's work with Boitano made such a difference that choreographers became all the rage in skating. And just how did Boitano do at the Olympics? Turn to the "Battle of the Brians" on page 60 and see!

Blueprint of a Program

Some choreographers draw detailed blueprints, or diagrams, on paper like this one. They map out every jump, spin, and step on the ice in time to the chosen music. Whether it was all the practicing or just the sheer love of it, Brian Boitano never forgot his Napoleon program. Years later, he was still able to draw a blueprint of it.

1. Start of Program
2. Start of Spiral Sequence
3. Combination Jump
4. Double Axel
5. Layback Spin
6. Combination Jump
7. Triple Toe Loop
8. Start of Footwork Sequence
9. Flying Sit Spin
10. End of Program

STARS

Ice dancing was never the same after Jayne Torvill and Christopher Dean rhumbaed onto the scene. The British dance team could evoke emotion, play characters, and tell stories through their programs like no skaters before. They choreographed most of their programs themselves with innovative moves that changed the steps of ice dancing. At the 1984 Olympics in Sarajevo, Yugoslavia, their free dance made figure skating history by earning a perfect set of artistry marks from all the judges.

Jayne Torvill and Christopher Dean

COSTUME PARADE THROUGH TIME

Figure skaters dress to kill the competition—and make an impression that judges won't forget. Even though the rules say costumes must not be "garish or theatrical in design," they are open to wide interpretation. Check out how skaters' costumes have developed and turned heads over the years.

Skate Bite

Scott Hamilton really lit up the ice. After turning pro, he once wore a costume that had battery-powered lights up and down the sides of his legs like tuxedo stripes.

1860s

Simply shocking! Not only does Jackson Haines skate to music (see page 24), he also wears fancy costumes to boot.

Jackson Haines

Late 1800s

Skaters bundle up to prevent frostbite. Ladies wear fashionable fitted jackets, ankle-length skirts trimmed with fur, and top it off with fur hats and muffs. *The Skaters Text Book* advises men to "leave off their overcoats" and women their corsets for the freedom to skate.

1908

Madge Syers competes in a long skirt, wide-brimmed hat, and billowing blouse. Male competitors wear leggings and bulky jackets with matching caps.

1924

The long skirt is gone for good when eleven-year-old Sonja Henie competes in a short skirt without petticoats so she can jump and spin.

1931

Boots are black or beige and European women wear stockings and bloomers to match the color of their boots. This creates an eye-pleasing line all the way from toe to waist and catches on around the world.

1948

The idea of skating in a costume takes root when American champ Dick Button wins the Worlds dressed in black pants and a white military jacket.

1950s

The "monkey suit" is born when a stretchy new body-hugging fabric is made into one-piece outfits for men. The suit comes only in black and is extremely hot and uncomfortable to wear.

1956

Glitter rocks the Olympics. U.S. skater Carol Heiss competes in an aqua chiffon dress with a rhinestone necklace and a sequined cap. Heiss wins the silver medal.

1964

Black and white is so boring, dudes! Monty Hoyt breaks the color code for men by wearing red pants at the U.S. championships.

1970s

Lycra and spandex are all the rage. The stretchy synthetic fabrics let skaters move more easily and jump higher. The result? Skaters add more rotations to jumps and spin in trickier positions.

Toller Cranston

1976

He's bizarre...he's exotic...he's Toller Cranston! Eyeballs pop at the Canadian champ's unusual artistic moves and unique stretchy jumpsuits with sequins.

1984

U.S. champ Scott Hamilton refuses to wear glitz at the Olympics. He opts for a costume like a speed-skating outfit to show he's an athlete. Hamilton wins gold, but few skaters follow suit.

1990s

Costumes become part of the "whole package" (see page 43). They're designed to reflect the music of skaters' programs, the character a skater is playing, or the mood skaters want to create.

Scott Hamilton

1994

Nancy Kerrigan outshines all her rivals in a white dress that sparkles with 11,500 rhinestones. Made by fashion designer Vera Wang, the dress costs a whopping $13,000. Luckily, the designer donates it to the U.S. champ.

Nancy Kerrigan

 Today

Skaters' costumes—such as those worn by American skater Johnny Weir—continue to shock, bend the rules, and help these athletes play characters by putting their best foot forward.

Costume No-Nos

Oh, no! Skaters' costumes are totally out of control. Maybe that's what the International Skating Union (ISU) thought after the 1988 season. Check out what some of the competitors wore:

- U.S. champion Debi Thomas raised eyebrows in a unitard—a tight-fitting one-piece costume that covered her body from neck to toe.

- Katarina Witt of East Germany outraged officials at the European Championships by wearing a costume cut high on the hips like a bathing suit. At the Calgary Olympics, she added feathers to cover up her hips.

- Czech champ Petr Barna went ape in a costume that bared his chest.

In 1989, the ISU made new rules. They banned unitards and bare midriffs. Costumes for women needed "skirts and pants covering the hips and posterior" and costumes for men needed "a neckline that does not expose the chest." They also banned "excessive decoration such as beads, sequins, feathers, and the like."

Turns out they were serious, too! At the 1994 U.S. Championships, Tonya Harding wore a costume with a neckline that plunged to her belly button. Not only did Tonya lose points, but the U.S. Figure Skating Association told her to get a different costume for the upcoming Olympics.

Skate Bite

Elite skaters wear makeup at competitions, so they don't look washed out under the bright lights of TV.

47

Sarah
Hughes

A Dream Performance

Sarah Hughes was in fourth place going into the long program at the 2002 Salt Lake City Olympics. A medal was within reach, but most people, including Sarah, didn't think she had a chance for gold.

"I thought there was no way in the world I could win," the American said. "So I just went out and just let it go." Skating before the top three women, Sarah opened with a dynamite double axel and a big smile. Next, she nailed a tough triple salchow-triple loop combination followed shortly by a perfect triple lutz and triple flip. The crowd went wild.

With infectious charm, she landed seven "triple ripples," flawlessly laying down the most technically difficult program in Olympic history. No one could match it. Sasha Cohen and Michelle Kwan both fell, and Irina Slutskaya left out her triple-triple. When all the marks were tallied, Sarah won the gold medal. And no one was more stunned than Sarah herself.

Chapter 7

JUDGMENT TIME

Boo! Hiss! If figure skating fans don't agree with the marks the judges give a skater, they speak their minds. And it's no wonder why. Picking the best figure skater is a matter of opinion and everyone's got one. It's just that it's the opinion of the judges that matters the most.

So just who are the judges? Some are former figure skaters, but others have never skated at all! They're just ordinary people with an extraordinary love of the sport. They've trained their eye to spot small differences in the performances of one skater from another.

But even judges can make mistakes. Some might say they're done on purpose. How have the judges managed to pull the Olympic podium out from under skaters' feet? And how is the new International Judging System designed to prevent that? Turn the page for the scoop.

Get the score on the judges

SCANDAL ROCKS THE RINK

What if you skated flawlessly, delivered a top-notch performance, and came in second to your main rivals who made mistakes? That was the story of Canadian pair Jamie Salé and David Pelletier at the 2002 Olympics. Here's how it shocked the world, exposed crooked judging, and gave the old judging system the boot.

Jamie Salé and David Pelletier

SIMPLY PERFECT?

When Jamie Salé and David Pelletier finished their free skate at the 2002 Olympics, the crowd went crazy. Skating without so much as a bobble or a wobble, the Canadian pair cast a magical spell over the ice with a flawless program. "It's got gold dust sprinkled all over it. It's one of the greatest skates in Olympic history," gushed one TV commentator. "Awesome!" "Simply perfect," said others. Fans and skating experts alike were sure Jamie and David had won the gold medal. Especially since their rivals, Russians Yelena Berezhnaya and Anton Sikharulidze, had slipped up a bit on their side-by-side double axels.

MARKS TO KISS-AND-CRY FOR

The crowd chanted "Six! Six! Six" as Jamie and David took seats in the "kiss-and-cry"—the spot where skaters wait for their marks. Under the old judging system, 6.0 was the mark of a perfect performance (see right). "5.8, 5.9, 5.8, 5.9…," the marks flashed across the screen, but not one 6.0 was in sight. Nobody could believe it. Five judges ranked Jamie and David second behind the Russians and only four put them first. The Canadians had lost the gold medal to the Russians in a five-to-four split decision. The crowd spat out a loud chorus of boos and hisses. "That [decision] will be debated forever," said one TV commentator.

A JUDGE CONFESSES

Sure enough, the story was far from over. That same night in a hotel lobby, the French judge, Marie-Reine Le Gougne, made a startling confession in front of some skating officials. She tearfully admitted that she had agreed to trade votes with the Russians! She had voted for their skaters in the pairs' competition and, in exchange, the Russian judge would vote for the French team in the ice dance. News of Le Gougne's confession broke fast, and outrage exploded around the world.

FUDGING IN JUDGING?

For years, people had charged that figure skating judging was open to fudging. As far back as the 1927 Worlds, there were rumblings that Norwegian skater Sonja Henie won only because three of the five judges were Norwegian. After that, the ISU made a rule that no country could have more than one judge on the judging panel. But still people complained that judges favored their own country. The French judge's jaw-dropping confession added fuel to this fire. So the ISU threw out the French vote, leaving a four-to-four tie and the Canadians with their own set of gold medals. That way, both pairs could share the golden victory. After the Olympics, the ISU brought in a new judging system (see next page). Is it any wonder that by that time Jamie, David, Yelena, and Anton had already decided to turn pro?

Salé, Pelletier, Berezhnaya, and Sikharulidze

The 6.0 System

In the old judging system, 6.0 was a mark to strive for. Judges awarded marks based on the following scale:

- 0.0 not skated
- 1.0 very poor
- 2.0 poor
- 3.0 mediocre
- 4.0 good
- 5.0 very good
- 6.0 perfect and faultless

A panel of nine judges each gave skaters two sets of marks—one for technical merit and the other for presentation. These two marks were then added together for a final score from each judge. This final score also gave skaters a rank, or placement, such as 1, 2, 3, and so on. Judges marked skaters carefully to ensure that the order of all their final scores, from highest to lowest, ranked the skaters from best to worst. A computer then used these rankings to calculate the winner.

Crooked Judging

The Fix Was In

Biff, boom, slide! French skater Jacqueline du Bief fell twice and slid across the rink on her tush at the 1952 Worlds. But that didn't stop the judges from awarding her the gold medal. The crowd trashed the ice in disgust with everything at hand, including glass bottles.

Tapping a Secret Code

Pssst, glance, tap. In 1999, TV footage showed two judges, Ukraine's Alfred Korytek and Russia's Sviatoslav Babenko, breaking the rules by talking, glancing, and tapping signals with their feet during the pairs' competition. Their votes for the top eight pairs were almost identical. Both judges were banned for a few years.

Wanna Trade Votes?

Brrring! Brrring! In between ice dancing events at the 1998 Olympics, Ukrainian judge Yuri Balkov phoned Canadian judge Jean Senft. Balkov wanted to swap votes—placing Canadian ice dancers third in exchange for Senft placing the Ukrainians eighth. Balkov said that judges from Lithuania and the Czech Republic were already in. Senft, who was recording the conversation, said no way. Later, when she exposed the tape, Balkov said the call was Senft's idea. The ISU suspended Balkov for a year—and Senft for six months!

HERE COME THE MARKS!

Want to wrap your head around the International Judging System (IJS) behind figure skating today? It takes two panels of fourteen experts and a whole lot of numbers and codes to try and call these events fair and square. And does it work? Read and judge for yourself!

JUDGES AT WORK

Nine judges sit on the judging panel at international competitions. Thanks to the new technical panel, the judges no longer have to identify the jumps and spins, or elements, skaters perform or even rank the skaters. The judges mark only the quality of skaters' moves and performances. To guard against cheating among the judges, a computer randomly discards a few of their scores, including the highest and lowest. Then the computer uses the rest of their scores to calculate the skaters' marks.

So which scores come from which judge? No one knows and that's the point—the judges are anonymous. In fact, the ISU rulebook says that the judges' room at competitions must have a shredder to destroy any papers used by a judge to figure out marks. The idea is that if people don't know how a judge has scored, they can never pressure one to favor a certain skater or pair of skaters. But many critics feel that by keeping the judges a mystery, the new system actually makes cheating easier!

TECHIES AT WORK

The technical panel has five experts. It's led by a technical specialist who calls, or identifies, each move as skaters perform them in real time. An assistant technical specialist and technical controller act like backup for the specialist. They help make sure all the calls are correct. Final calls are based on the majority of opinion. A video replay operator records all the elements skaters perform, so the panel and the judges may review them if needed. Finally, a data operator enters all the calls so they pop up on judges' computers. Whew!

TIP

How can you judge the quality of a spin? Look for a little pile of snow near the skater's blade on the ice. If the skater moves away from this snow pile, he is traveling. A skater can wander as much as 1.5 m (5 ft.) in a lousy spin!

THE SCORE SHEET

Each skater gets a score sheet like this one so they can see the details of their final score. What does it all mean? Check out Evgeni Plushenko's Olympic winning scores to find out!

Evgeni Plushenko

Rank Evgeni placed first in the free skate.

NOC Code Evgeni is from Russia. So the "name of country" code is RUS.

Base Value In this system, each jump, spin, and step has a pre-set value. Evgeni earned 14.5 points for his quadruple toeloop-triple toeloop-double loop jump combination.

GOE This stands for Grade of Execution. Judges score the quality of each jump and spin by giving it a "grade of execution" between +3 and -3. Each of these grades are added or subtracted from the base value.

Executed Elements These are the elements—jumps, spins, and steps— that Evgeni did in his program.

4T+3T+2Lo Every element gets a code like this. The numbers say how many revolutions were done and the letters stand for the type of move. This says that Evgeni began his program with a quadruple toeloop-triple toeloop-double loop jump combination. *Can you figure out what he did for his next five elements from the codes below? Hint: They are all jumps. (See answers page 64)*

Total Segment Score This score is calculated by adding the Total Element Score and Total Program Component Score. Then the scores for the free skate and the short program are added together, and the highest total wins!

FIGURE SKATING
PATINAGE ARTISTIQUE

MEN
HOMMES

FREE SKATING
PROGRAMME LIBRE

torino 2006

JUDGES DETAILS PER SKATER / NOTATION DÉTAILLÉE DES JUGES
PALAVELA   THU 16 FEB 2006 / JEU 16 FEV 2006

Rank	Name	NOC Code	Total Segment Score =	Total Element Score +	Total Program Component Score (factored) +	Total Deductions -
1	PLUSHENKO Evgeni	RUS	167.67	85.25	82.42	0.00

#	Executed Elements	Base Value	GOE	The Judges Panel (in random order)												Scores of Panel
1	4T+3T+2Lo	14.5	0.86	2	2	1	2	1	1	1	0	0	0	1	0	15.36
2	3A+2T	8.8	1.29	1	2	1	2	2	2	1	1	1	2	1		10.09
3	3Lo	5.0	0.86	1	1	2	1	0	2	1	0	1	0	1	1	5.86
4	3A	7.5	1.43	2	2	2	2	1	2	1	1	2	1	1	1	8.93
5	3Lz	6.0	1.00	1	1	1	1	1	1	2	0	1	0	1	1	7.00
6	3Lz+2T	7.3	0.71	1	0	1	0	1	1	1	0	0	0	1	1	8.01
7	CCoSp4	3.5	0.50	1	1	2	1	1	1	1	1	1	1	1	1	4.00
8	FCSp3	2.3	0.21	0	0	1	0	0	1	0	0	1	1	1	0	2.51
9	CiSt4	3.4	1.86	2	2	2	2	2	2	2	2	2	1	1	1	5.26
10	2F	1.9 x	0.00	0	0	0	-1	0	0	0	0	0	0	0	-1	1.90
11	3S	5.0 x	0.43	1	1	1	0	0	1	0	0	1	0	0	0	5.43
12	SlSt3	3.1	1.00	2	2	3	1	2	2	1	1	2	2	2	2	4.10
13	FSSp3	2.3	0.29	1	0	1	0	1	0	0	0	1	0	1	0	2.59
14	CCoSp4	3.5	0.71	1	2	2	1	1	1	0	1	2	2	1	1	4.21
		74.1														**85.25**

Program Components	Factor													Scores
Skating Skills	2.00	8.50	8.50	8.75	8.50	8.75	8.25	7.75	8.25	8.75	8.50	8.25	8.00	8.46
Transitions / Linking Footwork	2.00	7.00	8.25	8.00	7.00	8.25	8.00	7.50	8.00	8.25	8.00	7.25	6.25	7.75
Performance / Execution	2.00	8.00	8.50	8.75	8.25	8.50	8.50	8.25	8.25	8.75	8.50	8.25	7.75	8.39
Choreography / Composition	2.00	7.75	8.50	8.25	7.75	8.50	8.25	7.75	8.25	8.50	8.25	8.25	7.50	8.18
Interpretation	2.00	8.00	8.75	8.50	8.50	8.50	8.75	8.50	8.25	8.50	8.75	8.50	7.25	8.43
Judges Total Program Component Score (factored)														**82.42**

Deductions:	Costume & Prop Violation:	0.00		Time Violation:	0.00		Music Violation:	0.00	**0.00**
	Illegal Element:	0.00		Falls:	0.00		Interruption in Excess:	0.00	

Rank	Name	NOC Code	Total Segment Score	Total Element Score	Total Program Component Score (factored)	Total Deductions

Program Components Judges also mark these five components of skaters' overall presentation on a scale of 1 to 10 with 10 being the highest.

Deductions Judges deduct points from skaters' scores for falls and breaking the rules for the music, costume, or length of a program.

The Judges Panel Scores are shown in random order to protect the judges. However, judges are not anonymous at U.S. events.

Shae-Lynn Bourne
and Victor Kraatz

Skating Against All Odds

Daring! Brilliant! Thrilling! That was the buzz on the ice about Shae-Lynn Bourne and Victor Kraatz. The Canadian dance team wowed crowds everywhere with whiz-bang footwork and hydroblading moves leaning out low over the ice. But no matter what they did, the dynamic duo could not win over the judges. Shae-Lynn and Victor earned bronze medals four times at the Worlds and placed fourth at the Olympics twice.

At the 1998 Olympics, their free dance got the whole building grooving. However, the judges did not budge and Shae-Lynn and Victor were stuck in fourth place, the same spot as before the free dance. Because ice dancing is the least technical figure skating event, many said the judging was the most corrupt, with winners maybe determined months in advance! Shae-Lynn and Victor had the courage to say they felt the judges had kept them out of the medals.

The ISU changed the rules, making it difficult for judges to cut deals. They decided to have different judges for each ice dancing event and to announce their names just minutes beforehand. After the scandal of the 2002 Olympics, they also revamped the judging system altogether (see page 52). Then nothing could hold back Shae-Lynn and Victor—not even the judges. The Canadian dance team finally won the 2003 World Championships.

Skate great!

That's the name of the game in competition. No matter how brilliantly and perfectly top skaters have practiced their program, the question on everyone's mind remains: Can they do it now when it counts? No one thinks about this more than the skaters themselves!

And that's just for the World Championships. When it comes to the Olympics, the amount of pressure doubles! Many of these athletes have been dreaming of Olympic gold for years. Now, they're finally there and the eyes of the whole world are watching 24/7—even at their practices. It's enough to make their heads spin, if they let it. Even world champions have been known to crumble under such enormous expectations. Check out what makes some skaters thrive and others wilt under the heat of competition.

Brian
Joubert

Be dazzled!

TAKE THE ICE ● ● ● ● ● ● ● ● ● ● ● ● ● ● ● ●

"The secret to competition is not letting mistakes take over. You have to fight the whole way through," world champion Brian Boitano once said. And he should know—after all, he fought the legendary "Battle of the Brians" (see page 60). Check out how elite skaters go into battle to take the ice.

Alexei Yagudin

SKATE NOW!

Skate and deliver! Many world-class skaters can do it in practice. But only top champions can do it in competition. Before the best ever get to the Olympics, they practice exactly as they want to perform. If they fall, they get up and carry on without missing a beat just like they need to in competition. That way they learn how to recover automatically from falls. Practicing this way also builds their confidence. Once they're on the ice, they deliver their best by bringing all their talents to bear. When Alexei Yagudin finished his free skate at the 2002 Olympics, he even pumped his fists in the air!

COACH PLANS THE ATTACK

Good coaches help skaters hang tough mentally through each competition. For starters, they try to keep everything as close as possible to a skater's routine at home. Coaches also map out a strategy for the season. They get feedback from judges about the skater's programs and watch how other skaters are performing. They advise their own skater when to pull back and when to push to the edge. They must know their skater well enough to bring out the best performance when it's needed most. Minutes before U.S. Champion Evan Lysacek took the ice to compete one time, coach Debbie Storey told him to "attack like a panther."

IT'S A JUNGLE OUT THERE

Zoom! Turn! Jump! Skaters practice in a large group at competitions, zigzagging around one another, and landing jumps everywhere. Maybe that's why skaters have some rules about "right of way." First off, the skater whose music is playing has the right of way—the other skaters must skate around him. Second, whoever is setting up for a jump has the right of way. Skaters also make eye contact with one another to signal which way they're going. Still, skaters have been known to try to throw off competitors' concentration by skating right up behind them. To add to the pressure, judges, TV cameras, fans, other competitors, and their coaches crowd the stands. So everyone knows if a skater's having trouble!

Evan Lysacek

LUCK OF DRAW

Will your favorite skater skate first, last, or somewhere in between? It all depends on the luck of the draw. A random draw determines the order of skaters for the short program. The results of the short program determine the order for the long program. The competitors in the lowest-placed group skate first, the second lowest-placed group skates next, and so on until the top-placed group skates last. Another draw determines the order of the skaters in each of these groups. Skaters have to deal with the draw as best they can. Some like to watch their competition in action, but others don't. Some even listen to music after they've performed to block out the crowd's cheers or gasps for their rivals. So what is a "lucky draw?" That depends. Brian Boitano used to like to skate first to put pressure on those who followed. However, Katarina Witt liked to skate last. Once she saw what others had done, she knew exactly what to do to win.

Skate Bite

Skaters check how their music sounds in the competition rink. Believe it or not, some skaters have discovered that their music plays faster, or slower, in different rinks!

Dealing With the Competition

Sometimes, dealing with the competition isn't always above board. Check out how some skaters have tried to derail their rivals.

Slash Her Boots

As Austrian Olympic champ Herma Planck-Szabo laced up her boots to compete at the 1926 Worlds, the soles nearly fell right off. Someone had slipped into her room the night before and slit her boots. Talk about cut-boot competition!

Run Her Down

In 1976, Dorothy Hamill won the Olympic gold medal. But she almost didn't make it to the rink. Before the Games in Austria, a car nearly ran her over. Hamill saw a competitor in the car and the competitor's coach behind the wheel. But she refused to reveal their names.

Psyche Him Out

When Brian Boitano arrived at the rink for the short program at the 1988 Olympics, a fellow skater said, "Hurry up and get your skates on! Everyone's going on the ice for the warm-up!" Brian panicked. But then he realized he had lots of time and that the competitor was trying to unnerve him.

KNOCK 'EM DEAD

When the pressure peaks at the Olympics, some skaters do not self-destruct or even lose their edge. They knock the competition dead in spite of it. Check out these unflappable athletes!

Murphy's Law on Ice

Ever heard of Murphy's Law that says "if something can go wrong, it will"? Check out some mishaps that have sent skaters scrambling at the last minute.

I Forgot My Skates!

The night before the 2007 Junior Worlds, Canadian Patrick Chan took his skates out of his bag to air them. They were really stinky! In the morning, he forgot to put them back and left for the rink. His mom had to hightail it back to their hotel to get them! She returned to the rink in the nick of time for Patrick to take the ice.

Hot Off the Flesh

Just before her free skate at the 2002 Olympics, American Sasha Cohen discovered she had no tights. Fumie Suguri of Japan had just come off the ice, so Sasha borrowed her tights.

THE CARMENS DUKE IT OUT

What if you and your arch-rival were skating to the same music—excerpts from the opera *Carmen*? That was the situation between Katarina Witt of East Germany and Debi Thomas of the U.S. at the 1988 Olympics. It was the "Battle of the Carmens" and things were tight. Debi placed second in figures with Katarina right behind her. Then Katarina won the short program and Debi came in second. Whichever "Carmen" won the free skate would win the gold medal. Katarina skated first. Her "Carmen" brought the house down. However, she changed her triple loop to a double, so Debi still had a shot. Debi missed her first combination jump and her "Carmen" began to unravel. Katarina nabbed the gold while Debi settled for bronze. On the podium, Debi would not even shake Katarina's hand. But Katarina wasn't offended at all. The competitor in her understood completely.

TOTALLY MENTAL

Paul Wylie was ready to hang up his skates for good. The American skater had just stepped out of two triple axels at the 1992 U.S. Nationals. He thought he'd blown his chance to the make the Olympic team. In competitions, his nerves always seemed to get the best of him. Then someone burst into the dressing room and told him he had made it onto the podium. He was going to the Olympics! Paul's attitude changed completely, focusing on everything positive. He slipped under everyone's radar at the Olympics and came in third in the short program. In reach of a medal, he didn't want to fold again under pressure. "The next day I went to the team sports psychologist and asked how I could keep from choking," Paul said. The psychologist told him to visualize all the details of what a medal would do for his career and then forget about it and focus on the free skate. Paul did just that, shocking the world and himself by winning the silver medal.

Honey, I Shrunk the Dress!

Joannie Rochette's mom washed her costumes before the 2006 Worlds and they shrunk! The skirt on the dress for Joannie's long program almost disappeared. Luckily, they were able to reach the costume designer in time and she made a new skirt.

SQUEEZING OUT THE COMPETITION

Tara Lipinski wanted to get everything she could out of the 1998 Olympics—including her competitors! The 15-year-old stayed in the athletes' village, chatted with the press, and even got Wayne Gretzky's autograph. "If I don't get an Olympic medal what am I left with?" she said. "I want my Olympic memories. This is my chance to have fun." Meanwhile, heavy favorite Michelle Kwan kept a low profile in a hotel. After the short program, Tara was in second place nipping at Michelle's heels. Then, Michelle took to the ice and laid down the gauntlet with a near-perfect long program. Her only glitch was a shaky landing on a triple flip. Talk about pressure! But Tara didn't buckle. She went out and nailed seven triples bang-on, grinning from ear to ear as she landed each one. Her joy flooded the entire building and nabbed her the gold medal!

STAR ·············

Mao Asada sparkles on the ice. The Japanese world champion is one of only a handful of women ever to land a triple axel in competition. What's more, she can do a biellmann spin, holding one leg up behind her head, with just one hand. Is it any wonder she makes people's heads spin?

Mao Asada

Quick Answers to Slippery Questions

Do guys need a quad?

Maybe yes and maybe no. Only a few skaters have ever landed a quad in competition. But nowadays, many people say guys shouldn't bother showing up without a quad. At the 2002 Olympics, all the medalists landed quads successfully. In fact, U.S. skater Timothy Goebel nailed three—more than anyone else—yet he won only bronze. He couldn't beat Russians Alexei Yagudin, who won gold, or Evgeni Plushenko, who won silver. What's more, in 2008, Canadian Jeffrey Buttle won the Worlds without even attempting a quad. At the time, he said he thought he'd need a quad for the Olympics though. After all, the Olympics are a competition like no other!

Are skaters superstitious?

You bet! Some skaters follow rituals for luck when they compete. Oksana Baiul always stepped onto the ice with her left skate. Brian Boitano always ate pasta the night before a competition. Michelle Kwan always wore a gold necklace with a Chinese dragon charm. Some research shows that superstitious rituals like these may help athletes deal with mental stress. And if skaters can calm their minds, it becomes much easier for them to perform at their best on the ice.

Brian Orser
and Brian Boitano

BRIAN
VS
BRIAN

The Battle of the Brians

"**B**oitano!" "Orser!" "Boitano!" "Orser!" The mighty battle between Canadian Brian Orser and American Brian Boitano at the 1988 Olympics in Calgary, Canada was as close as they come. Neck-and-neck through the figures and short programs, each knew that if he made a mistake, the other Brian would probably win.

Boitano's program began with his 'tano triple lutz (see page 45) and a triple axel-triple toe loop. The crowd was transfixed, but he felt he needed something extra to win. With one last burst, he closed with another triple axel and touched down perfectly with a huge grin. Off the ice, Orser heard the cheers for Boitano. The pressure was now all on his program.

Orser started beautifully, but then stepped out of a triple flip. Still he held on. If only he could do everything else cleanly! Not knowing that Boitano had done two triple axels, he made his second triple only a double. When the marks arrived, Boitano had edged Orser by just one-tenth of a point! Under huge pressure, Boitano had skated his best. And that's what made him a champion.

Single and Pair Skating

Single skaters skate in separate competitions for men and women, er, ladies. That's right—their competition is called the ladies' competition just like the first figure skating competition for women more than one hundred years ago! In pair skating, a man and woman compete as a team. Single and pair competitions have two parts of equal weight, or value:

Short Program

• Must be two minutes and fifty seconds long or less, or points are deducted.

• Skaters must perform eight required elements, such as a triple axel jump, layback spin, or lift.

• Skaters receive points for each of the elements they perform. Judges add or subtract points for the quality of execution of each and deduct points for any falls or rule violations.

• Judges also mark skaters' overall presentation, or program components.

• A computer gives equal weight to the total element score and total program component score then adds the scores together for the short program score.

Free Skate or Long Program

• Must be four minutes long for women and four minutes and thirty seconds long for men and pairs, give or take ten seconds, or points are deducted.

• Skaters may include any elements they wish as long as they meet the ISU's requirements for a well-balanced program, such as a maximum of eight jumps, three spins, or two throw jumps.

• Skaters receive points and scores in the same way as the short program.

And the Winner Is…

• A computer adds up skaters' scores for the short program and free skate and the skater or pair with the most points wins the competition.

• If two or more skaters, or pairs, have the same number of points, the one who scored the most points in the free skate wins.

Ice Dance

A man and woman skate together, competing as a dance team. The competition has three parts of equal weight:

Compulsory Dances

• Each year the ISU chooses two dances that all dance teams must perform to the same music with the same steps.

• Dance teams receive points for technical elements they perform, such as steps, turns, and movements. Judges add and subtract points for the quality of execution of each technical element.

• Judges also mark the following components of the whole performance: skating skills, performance or execution, interpretation, and timing.

• A computer gives the timing and skating skills scores the most weight, adds component scores together and adds this total to the technical score.

Original Dance

• Dance teams skate a program of original choreography to music they choose that fits a rhythm, or character, chosen by the ISU every year.

• Dance teams receive scores in the same way as the compulsory dances. In addition, judges mark the transitions, or linking footwork, and choreography of the whole performance.

• A computer gives the interpretation score the most weight among the component scores then adds the component scores together and adds the total to the technical score.

Free Dance

• Must be four minutes long, give or take ten seconds, or points will be deducted.

• Dance teams skate a creative program of dance steps and movements to express the character of the music of their choice.

• Dance teams receive scores in the same way as the original dance.

• A computer gives the transitions and skating skills the most weight in the component scores then adds component scores together and adds the total to the technical score.

And the Winner Is…

• A computer adds up the scores for all dances. The team with the highest number of points wins.

• If two or more dance teams have the same number of points, the team who scored the most points in the free dance wins.

SKATE TALK

6.0 System — the old judging system in which skaters' marks ranged from 0.0 for "not skating" a program to 6.0 for a "perfect and faultless" program.

Amateur — a skater who participates and competes without being paid (see Professional).

Approach — how a skater enters a jump, including footwork and his or her body position.

Axel jump — named for its inventor Axel Paulsen, a jump in which skaters take off from an outside edge skating forward and land on the opposite foot skating backward. To go from skating forward to backward like this requires half a revolution more in the air than any other jump.

Base value — the number of points a jump, spin, or step is worth, depending on level of difficulty, before points are added or removed for grade of execution.

Biellmann spin — an upright spin, named for its inventor Denise Biellmann, in which a skater extends one leg up behind and over her head and holds onto the skate blade with both hands.

Blade — the thin metal part of an ice skate that contacts the ice.

Boot — the bootlike part of a skate covering the foot and ankle.

Camel spin — a spin in which the skating leg is straight and the free leg is extended parallel to the ice so that the legs form a right angle. The torso is parallel to the ice.

Choreography — the art of putting movements together to interpret music.

Combination — two or more jumps done one after the other without any steps in between, or two or more spins done one after the other without stopping.

Crossovers — skating strokes in which one foot crosses over the other to skate forward or backward.

Death drop — a jump during which a skater's body is briefly parallel to the ice before it drops into a sit spin.

Death spiral — a pair move in which the man pivots on one foot, holding the woman by one hand, as she circles around him on one skate blade with her body parallel and low to the ice.

Deduction — points that judges take away from skaters' scores for falling or breaking rules.

Doing a Midori — jumping so close to the boards that you land in the stands like Japanese champion Midori Ito once did in world competition.

Double — a jump with two revolutions in the air.

Doubled — did a double jump instead of a triple or quadruple.

Edges — the two sharp sides of a skate blade that skaters use to grip the ice.

Edge jumps — jumps in which a skater takes off from the edge of a skate blade without touching the ice with the other foot.

Element — a jump, spin, or step in a skater's program.

Figures — shapes or patterns, like the number eight, that skaters trace on the ice with their skate blades to demonstrate skill; figure skating gets its name from this event, but figures are no longer part of competitions.

Flip jump — when a skater uses a toe pick boost to take off from the inside edge of one foot, turn one to four times in the air, and land on the opposite foot.

Flying spin — a spin that skaters enter by jumping into the air.

Flutz — when a skater sets up for a lutz jump but changes the takeoff edge from outside to inside at the last second. This results in a flip jump, which is easier than a lutz.

Free leg or foot — a skater's leg, or foot, not in contact with the ice.

Footwork — a number of related steps, hops, turns, and changes of position that come one after another.

Grade of Execution (GOE) — a score, anywhere from +3 to -3 points, that a judge gives for the quality of a jump or spin; the GOE is added to or subtracted from the base value (number of points) of the jump or spin.

Hollow — the groove that runs the length of a skate blade creating an edge on either side.

Ice dance — a type of figure skating in which a man and woman use intricate footwork and movements to "dance" on ice, expressing the rhythm and the mood of different types of music.

International Judging System (IJS) — the current judging system in which skaters receive points for each technical element they perform, such as a jump or spin, as well as overall presentation.

International Skating Union (ISU) — the group, or organization, that runs international figure skating competitions and makes the rules for the sport.

Interpretation — the ability of skaters to express the mood, emotions, and character of music through moves and steps on the ice.

Judge — an official who marks, or grades, skaters' performances.

Jump — a move in which skaters leap into the air and complete one to four revolutions before landing on the ice on one foot.

Landing — when a skater finishes a jump by touching down on the ice on one foot.

Layback spin — an upright spin in which a skater arches her back and drops her head and shoulders backward.

Lift — a pairs move in which the man raises his partner above his head.

Loop jump — when a skater takes off from the outside edge of one foot, turns one to four times in the air, and lands on the same edge.

Lutz jump — named for its inventor Alois Lutz. In this jump, a skater gets a toepick boost to takeoff from the outside edge of one foot, turns one to four times in the air, and lands on the opposite foot.

Marks — the scores given by the judging panel to grade a skater's performance.

Pivot — a two-foot spin with one foot planted in the ice.

Presentation mark — in the 6.0 judging system, this was the second set of marks that judges gave skaters, often called "artistic impression" or the artistic mark; today judges mark skaters' "overall presentation" (see Program Components below).

Professional — an elite skater who has retired from amateur, or unpaid, skating events, such as the World Championships and Olympic Games, and is paid to perform in ice skating shows and competitions.

Program — a performance composed of choreography and jumps and spins done in time to music.

Program Components — the five parts of a program's presentation that judges mark—skating skills, transitions or linking footwork, performance or execution, choreography, and interpretation.

Quad — short for quadruple, a jump with four revolutions in the air.

Referee — an official who supervises the judges during competitions.

Required elements — jumps, spins, or footwork that skaters must perform in the short program, original dance, or free dance. The ISU makes the list of required elements and changes the list each year.

Revolution — a full-circle turn, especially in the air.

Salchow jump — named for its inventor Ulrich Salchow. In this jump, a skater takes off from the inside edge of one foot, turns one to four times in the air, and lands on the opposite foot's outside edge.

Sequence — a connected set of steps or moves performed in time to the music.

Serpentine — footwork that curves back and forth across the ice like a serpent.

Single — a jump with one revolution in the air; also a branch of figure skating in which women or men skate alone.

Sit spin — a spin in the sitting position on one leg with the other leg extended straight out.

Skate Canada — the group, or organization, that runs competitive skating in Canada, including national competitions.

Skating foot — the foot in contact with the ice.

Spin — a move in which a skater whirls around quickly in one spot on the ice.

Spiral — a long glide in which a skater bends forward at the waist and extends one leg out behind.

Spread eagle — a glide in which a skater points both feet out to the sides in opposite directions with straight legs that form an upside down "V" shape.

Stroking — skating by pushing off the inside edge of first one skate then the other.

Technical Controller — the leader of the technical panel of officials who identify and videotape the jumps, spins, and steps that skaters perform during competition.

Technical Specialist — an official who identifies each jump and spin as skaters are performing them.

Tempo — the speed at which music plays.

Tests — when skaters perform moves in front of judges to demonstrate their skills to move up, or advance, through the competitive levels of figure skating.

Throw jump — a pairs move in which the male lifts and throws his partner across the ice. She turns one to four times in the air and lands on one foot.

Timing — the ability of a couple to skate in time with the music and the rhythm of the beat.

Toe jump — jump in which a skater begins by pushing off the toepick of one skate.

Toe loop jump — a jump in which a skater uses a toe pick boost to take off, and lands on the outside edge of the same foot.

Toe pick — the teeth or points at the front of a skate blade.

Total Segment Score — the total number of points a skater gets in a particular part of competition.

Tracings — the marks skate blades leave on the ice.

Triple — a jump with three revolutions in the air.

Twist — a pair move in which the man lifts and releases the woman into the air. She rotates up to three and half times as he does a half turn on the ice. He then catches her and lowers her to the ice.

United States Figure Skating Association (USFSA) — the group, or organization, that runs competitive skating in the United States, including national competitions.

Visualization — imagining, or mentally rehearsing, moves, such as jumps and spins, so you can instinctively do them in competition successfully.

The Whole Package — top notch jumps and spins combined with excellent presentation, interpretation of music, and choice of costume to create a mood or tell a story.

World Championships — a skating competition held every year among the top amateur skaters from countries around the world.

Zamboni — a machine that cleans and smoothes the ice.

INDEX

Photo Credits

Care has been taken to trace ownership of copyright material contained in this book. Information enabling the publisher to rectify any reference or credit line in future editions will be welcomed.

Roger Yip: Front and back cover, 2–3, 5 (boy), 7, 27, 29, 35, 36; Steve MacEachern: Ice backgrounds; Lucy Nicholson/Reuters: 4, 55; Reuters Photographer/Reuters: 5 (Kwan), 6, 11, 34, 45 (Torvill & Dean), 50, 52, 54, 56 (Yagudin); Detroit's Olympic Stadium by Robert Wimmer. Available from the publisher online at www.arcadiapublishing.com or by calling 888-313-2665: 13; Canada's Sports Hall of Fame: 14; Fibobjects/Dreamstime.com: 15; Dr. Federico Formenti, University of Oxford: 16 (bone skate); Cheryl Fenton: 16 (wooden skate); Helena Grigar: 16 (Haines); AP Photo/CP Images: 17 (Henie); Courtesy of Kathy Atkinson/University of Delaware: 17 (skate); Lee Jinman/AP Photo: 17 (Beacom); Skate Canada Archives: 17 (Wagner & Paul), 20, 23 (Schuba with gold), 24 (Dafoe & Bowden), 24 (Jackson), 25 (Bourne & Kraatz), 25 (Eisler & Brasseur), 46 (Haines); Image Club Graphics disc: 18; David Gray/Reuters: 21; The Fourth Olympiad 1908 London Official Report published by The British Olympic Association in 1909: 22, 24 (Salchow); © CIO/Auguste Couttet: 23 (Joly & Brunet); Bob Strong/Reuters: 25 (Ando); Harry Harris/AP Photo: 26; Thomas Kienzle/AP Photo: 31; Pub Domain/Wikipedia Commons: 37 (Pavlova); Courtesy of sashacohen.com: 37 (Cohen); Kevork Djansezian/AP Images: 38; Jo Yong hak/Reuters: 39; F.Scott Grant/Skate Canada: 40; PC Photo/AOC/CP Images: 41, 47 (Hamilton), 60; Gérard Châtaigneau, FSC-SportIms: 42; Mike Cassese/Reuters: 43; John Redman/AP Photo/CP Images: 45 (Boitano); Graham Bezant/CP Images: 46 (Cranston); Lionel Cironneau/AP Images: 47 (Kerrigan); Doug Mills/AP Images: 48; Martin Meissner/CP Images: 49; Amy Sancetta/AP Images: 51; David Gray/Reuters: 53; Eriko Sugita/Reuters: 56 (Lysacek); Caroline Paré: 59.

Answers

Try This page 8: Chances are the two ice cubes stuck together. Way back in 1850, scientist Michael Faraday suggested that this happens because a thin film of water covers ice. When two pieces of ice come in contact, this layer freezes and fuses the pieces together. 150 years later, scientists found evidence to support Faraday's theory.

Try This page 22: Does your tracing look like an 8? If you were able to push off with the same amount of speed with each foot *and* tilt your skate blades the exact same amount on each foot, the two circles of your tracing should be perfectly round.

Spot the Spin, page 29: 1=C, 2=A, 3=B

Try This page 29: Did you notice that as you brought your arms to your chest, you began to spin faster? As all objects spin, their weight presses out from the center. Skaters use this rule to control how fast they spin. To speed up, they draw their arms and legs in close to their bodies. To slow down, they hold their arms and legs out.

Evgeni jumps, Page 53: 2 3A+2T (triple axel-double toe loop jump combination), 3 3Lo (triple loop), 4 3A (triple axel), 5 3Lz (triple lutz), 6 3Lz+DT (triple lutz-double toe loop jump combination)